CAPitalize Your Sales

Endorsements

"Chris Panagiotu's *Capitalize Your Sales* is a must-read for anyone serious about excelling in sales and life. When I started out in my career, I learned the power of classic sales books like *How I Raised Myself from Failure to Success Through Selling* by Frank Bettger, *Think and Grow Rich* by Napoleon Hill, and *How to Win Friends and Influence People* by Dale Carnegie. Chris's book stands proudly among these greats but with a modern twist—it's packed with updated, practical advice tailored for today's digital era. Chris brings a vibrant energy to his writing, making it not just a guide but a source of inspiration. If you're looking to get ahead, gain clients, and find success through relationships, this book should be on your shelves. It's a book I wish I would have had to read when I was starting out."

~**Guy Spier,** Lead Investor of AquaMarine Fund and bestselling author of *The Education of a Value Investor*

"Chris brings readers inside a real and intentional journey towards sales success. *CAPitatlize Your Sales* emphasizes authentic details on the path to $1,000,000 in an easy to read and principled to practice formula. I'm excited for those looking to level up their sales game and impact along the way."

~**Alec Ingold,** Miami Dolphins Fullback, Walter Payton Man of the Year Nominee and Amazon bestselling author of *The Seven Crucibles*

"Chris Panagiotu's infections energy and boundless enthusiasm are truly remarkable. His passion for helping others shines through inspiring everyone to take action and achieve their goals."
~**Nick Hutchison,** Founder of BookThinkers and bestselling author of *Rise of the Reader*

"No matter what your profession is, selling your idea is the key to success. Do yourself and your business a favor and let Chris Panagiotu take you by the hand and show you how the best gets the job done."
~**Robert Hagstrom,** New York Times bestselling author of *The Warren Buffett Way*, author of *The Warren Buffett Portfolio* and Chief Investment Officer at EquityCompass

"There's an old forgotten adage that goes like this; nothing in this world ever happens without something first being sold. In today's ever more competitive world, that statement is even more true today. Chris cuts through the clutter to bring you practical, user-friendly advice that you can implement today to take your company to heights you could never imagine!"
~**Ken Rusk,** author of *Blue Collar Cash*

"*CAPitalize Your Sales* is a must-read primer for anyone who wants to level up their skills. Read this book to learn from one of the best."
~ **Laurie Barkman,** founder of Business Transition Sherpa LLC, adjunct professor at Carnegie Mellon, and author of *The Business Transition Handbook*

"CAPitalize Your Sales is an amazing book that will powerfully change the way you do business if you are wise enough to follow its advice."

~**Gautam Baid,** bestselling author of
The Joys of Compounding

"CAPitalize Your Sales is a masterful guide to achieving success in sales. Chris Panagiotu's emphasis on building genuine relationships and understanding your purpose provides a solid foundation for long-term success. Filled with examples, stories, and "do-this-now" tools, it's like having an extended lunch with the sales mentor you wish you had. An essential read for sales professionals at any level."

~**David Newman,** bestselling author of
Do It! Marketing and *Do It! Selling*

"Chris serves as a powerful guide in the fast-paced world of finances that leads from a values-based perspective. He has a relational and authentic voice that makes you feel like you have a committed partner in your corner that not only supports sound investing but leads to financial freedom. His passion to see you succeed comes through on every page."

~**Dr. Heather Penny,** author of
Grace Space, The Life You're Made For,
The Life You're Made For Coaching Companion
and *The Bracelet*

"Chris takes readers on a guided, exciting and entertaining adventure into his journey from $0 to $1,000,000 in a way that makes success easy and accessible for those looking to level up their sales craft with utmost sincerity."

~**Brian Covey,** EVP Revolution Mortgage

CAPITALIZE *your* SALES

The All-In-One Sales Framework that Saves You from Ever Struggling Again & Teaches You How to Sell with Sincerity

CHRISTOPHER A. PANAGIOTU

NEW YORK

LONDON • NASHVILLE • MELBOURNE • VANCOUVER

CAPitalize Your Sales

The All-In-One Sales Framework that Saves You from Ever Struggling Again and Teaches You How to Sell with Sincerity

© 2025 Christopher A. Panagiotu

All rights reserved. No portion of this book may be reproduced, stored in a retrieval system, or transmitted in any form or by any means—electronic, mechanical, photocopy, recording, scanning, or other—except for brief quotations in critical reviews or articles, without the prior written permission of the publisher.

Published in New York, New York, by Morgan James Publishing. Morgan James is a trademark of Morgan James, LLC. www.MorganJamesPublishing.com

Proudly distributed by Publishers Group West®

ISBN 9781636984766 paperback
ISBN 9781636984773 ebook
Library of Congress Control Number: 2024941122

Cover & Interior Design by:
Christopher Kirk
www.GFSstudio.com

Morgan James is a proud partner of Habitat for Humanity Peninsula and Greater Williamsburg. Partners in building since 2006.

Get involved today! Visit: www.morgan-james-publishing.com/giving-back

Table of Contents

Foreword xi
Preface: How I Became a CAPitalizer xv

Chapter 1:   What is Your Purpose? 1

SECTION 1: **Get them into your "office"** 9
Chapter 2:   CAPitalize on Networking Events 15
Chapter 3:   CAPitalize on "Cold" Calling (off the networking event) 27
Chapter 4:   CAPitalize on "Out-and-About" Selling 33
Chapter 5:   CAPitalize on Social Media Sales 39

SECTION 2: **What to do to make them a client** 47
Chapter 6:   The three types of people you NEED to know 51
Chapter 7:   The Initial Meeting 61
Chapter 8:   How to conduct a presentation meeting 71
Chapter 9:   Now that they're a client, keep them coming back! 79

SECTION 3: How to build a top tier referral pipeline 85

Chapter 10:	Now that you have clients, learn who helps in making them succeed...and partner with them!	91
Chapter 11:	"Warm" calling to set up meetings with your soon-to-be new business partners	97
Chapter 12:	Your top referral source is in front of you: now what?	105
Chapter 13:	How to keep the good times (and referrals) rolling: the 90-day cheat code	115

SECTION 4: Now that you've made it, become the best of the best 127

Chapter 14:	Transform from sales expert to CEO	131
Chapter 15:	Learn the power of outsourcing........................	137
Chapter 16:	When it's time to *stop* reinvesting into your framework (and instead invest in yourself)........................	145
Chapter 17:	Why am I doing this?	151

Tools to keep you on track in CAPitalizing Your Sales 157

Acknowledgments.. 167

References 171

Foreword

When Christopher Panagiotu asked me to write the foreword for his new book, *CAPitalize Your Sales*, I'll admit—I almost said no. Now, before you gasp, let me explain. You see, I've never really considered myself strong in sales. I've always admired those who could sell ice to an Eskimo, but I never thought I was one of those people. Traditional sales advice never really resonated with me. So, when Chris offered, I had to ask him, "Why me?" And in true Chris fashion, he was honest, kind, and completely genuine. He said that I was the perfect person to write this foreword because of my focus on sincere selling, building genuine connections, and creating lasting relationships—exactly what this book represents. And that's when it clicked—I was perfect for this foreword. And if Chris Panagiotu thinks you're perfect for something, well, you just say yes, because this guy knows how to spot potential like nobody else!

Let me take you back to when I first met Chris. It was nearly two years ago through a mutual friend and colleague, Nick

Hutchison, founder of Book Thinkers and the author of *Rise of the Reader*. I was working with Nick to promote my book, *The Comfort Zone*, and he introduced me to Chris who was also working to promote his first book, *CAPitalize Your Finances*. From our first conversation, Chris and I just clicked—like we'd known each other for years. We share similar values—faith, integrity, and a commitment to helping others—and it didn't take long for our friendship to grow. We stayed in touch, and not long after, I had the pleasure of being a guest on his incredible podcast, *CAPitalize Your Finances Podcast*. We had an amazing conversation about how expanding your comfort zone can lead to growth—not just in life, but in finances as well. And let me tell you, Chris knows a thing or two about capitalizing on your finances. Right? Of course!

I finally met Chris in person in September at the *Book Thinkers Meetup* and the Lewis Howes *Summit of Greatness* event weekend. It was like meeting up with an old friend—we talked, we laughed, and we had dinner with other mutual friends. I remember thinking, "This guy is the real deal." He's the kind of person who makes you feel like you're the only person in the room, even when you're surrounded by hundreds of people. Since then, Chris and I have kept in touch, and I've had the joy of watching him grow, not just professionally but personally too. Chris recently became a dad, and let me tell you, the pictures he sends of his daughter together with his wife are beyond adorable. I'm pretty sure she's going to grow up to be just as charismatic as her dad. His love and pride for his family are one of the many things that make Chris who he is—a man of integrity, kindness, and heart.

Now, let's talk about Chris and capitalizing on sales. Chris is someone who truly understands the value of building authentic relationships. He's not about making a quick buck—he's about creating lasting connections that are built on trust and mutual respect. He believes in understanding your purpose before making a sale, aligning with his philosophy that true success comes from connecting with others on a deeper level. He knows that being genuine, helpful, and attracting the right people who know your worth are the keys to success. And, let me just say, in a world where sales can sometimes feel cold and transactional, Chris's approach is a breath of fresh air. He combines modern strategies with timeless values, making his approach both effective and lifelong. Chris's approach to selling, much like his approach to finance, is infused with his characteristic humor and authenticity, making the process less intimidating and more about building real, lasting connections.

CAPitalize Your Sales isn't just a book about increasing your numbers—it's a book about transforming your life and your business through genuine, heartfelt connections. Chris has an infectious personality—he's caring, funny, and one of the most honorable people I know. His integrity shines through in everything he does, and it's one of the reasons he's been so successful. This book will walk you through the steps of sincere networking, mastering the initial meeting, and keeping clients coming back, all while building a top-tier referral pipeline. When you read this book, you're not just getting sales advice—you're getting a masterclass on how to build relationships that last, how to be true to yourself in every interaction, and how to sell with sincerity.

Chris has shown me what it means to truly capitalize on life, and I am grateful for that. Whether it's his spiffy new office downtown, which he proudly showed me on Zoom (and yes, it's as impressive as it sounds), or the way he balances his professional success with his deep commitment to his family and faith, Chris is someone who lives what he preaches. He teaches that sales aren't just about closing deals—they're about opening doors, building bridges, and creating opportunities for others to succeed alongside you.

So, as you dive into this book, know that you're in for a transformative experience. Chris Panagiotu isn't just teaching you how to sell; he's showing you how to lead with integrity, build relationships that matter, and create a life you can be proud of. He's one of the most stand-up guys I know, and I'm honored to call him a good friend.

Get ready to become a CAPitalizer on your sales, your business, and your life. Let's go!

By Kristen Butler
Founder and CEO of Power of Positivity,
Entrepreneur, Keynote Speaker and
3x Best Selling Author of *3 Minute Positivity Journal,
3 Minute Happiness Journal* and *The Key to Positivity*

Preface:
How I Became a CAPitalizer

Welcome to CAPitalize Your Sales! This is going to be one heck of a read for those of you who are looking to master your salesmanship, but before we dive into the nitty-gritty, I first want to give you the backstory of what got me to this point of wanting to share this God-given gift of understanding everything one needs to know about sincere selling.

For those of you who have followed my career, whether directly through my financial planning business or indirectly through my podcast, my first book CAPitalize Your Finances, or my first masterclass on financially planning for yourself, you are well aware that I am a tremendous proponent of giving credit where credit is due. In the world of finance, I have been tremendously blessed with a combination of wise mentors, intelligent investors, and processes that I can continue to clone and tweak to my framework. There are dozens if not hundreds of individuals who have directly and indirectly guided me through understanding the true world of personal finance, and if I had to thank every person who made my first installment of knowledge possible, I would have to write another book solely devoted to dedications! In the world of money, there are so many moving parts, and when it comes to understanding what you need to do, it's mission critical that you stay within your bumpers and "stick with your salsa" (I explain this concept in depth in my first book, CAPitalize Your Finances). I say all of this because in the world of sales, although I had people behind the scenes inspiring me to succeed, at the end of the day, unlike the world of money, the objective is quite simple:

Get out there and figure it out.

If you are reading the sentence above and feel nervous, here's a breath of fresh air: don't be! You have THE book that will guide you every step of the way so you don't have to ask yourself "what do I do next?"

My guess is that, at this point, you are anxious and ready to get going on CAPitalizing Your Sales, but be a bit more patient. I want to take the time to give you some background on who the heck I am because once you know my backstory, you will realize that if I can do what I have done in my career (don't worry, you number lovers...we will get into that shortly... remember... patience!), anyone can achieve success in their sales process. So with that, here comes the background on Christopher A. Panagiotu, The CAP in CAPitalize!

Growing up, I always wanted to be financially successful. This is one of the reasons why I chose my profession, but after twenty-three years of investing, seventeen years of advising and nearly ten years of enlightening people on what it means to CAPitalize on their Finances, I can say that it would not have mattered what profession I chose (and it shouldn't matter for you either). Just like any industry, when I started off my career as an EXTREMELY green financial advisor at the largest wealth management firm in the world, I could not have been more naïve. Listen to this: I thought that by simply working at this massive conglomerate, wearing a suit and tie, and sounding like I remotely knew what I was talking about was going to instantly catapult me to financial success. Spoiler alert: that dream lasted +/- 20 seconds. The good news with my situation was, despite my naivete, my greenness was shielded by the fact that at the time, I was going to college full time, so the whole idea of getting out there to sell took a HARD backseat. After graduation and transitioning out of the largest wealth management firm to the second largest wealth management firm, I quickly—and we are talking lightning speed—discovered my first assumption of leaning on a big firm name was NOT going to get me to the promised land financially, professionally, or personally.

Strike two was my compounded naivete in deciding to start what is now my financial planning business out of my apartment May 12, 2015, with two non-competes, no real network and—even better—no real office! Take a moment and put yourself in my situation at the time: nearly twenty-three years old, no office, no network and...frankly...no practical hope of succeeding. Could you imagine meeting a guy like me back in the day and saying "Twenty-three years old with no office and nobody has ever heard of this guy: THIS is the guy I will entrust with my life's savings." It was a tough sell...trust me. In the world of finance, contrary to popular belief, there is zero coaching on sincere salesmanship. Reread that sentence if you didn't catch that. Is there coaching on how to sell? Absolutely, but it is NOT what is going to make you succeed in the long run. Techniques like backing up the wagon, luring money in on one's emotional lack of sophistication with investing, answering what you're asked even though it's not the full answer to the question the customer asked in the first place: these are a few of the MANY strategies that I was taught at the start of my career. There's a saying that I like to remind my followers of, time after time: a short-term gain is a long-term pain (and it works both ways). I quickly learned that not only were these techniques going to lead me down the path of failure, but I would be compromising my character and goodwill, which are the two most valuable assets one can own.

The good news with my new situation was I had zero subconscious negative influence from the "powers that be" lurking behind my shoulders. There was one major problem: I also had zero true sales training or experience. I knew what did not work (which is a valuable mental model for you to implement if you haven't already done so in your life), but that only gets you so far when you are nearly broke and need to make a living immediately.

One of the first thoughts that hopped into my brain was to do what just about anyone does these days: get on Google and look up sales training and coaching, whether it was one-on-one with an "expert" or books that could guide me and deliver the magic formula that would take me from financially empty to a mountain of wealth. News flash: there was not one book out there that laid it out for me in practical detail and the coaches were costly and SUPER salesy...which, now that I think about it...is kind of the point...but you get where I am coming from! What stunned me was the coaches never gave their backstory, so how in the world was I able to truly trust their judgement when I couldn't even find out if their story or stories were legit?! Unlike the world of finance where there was (to most people's detriment), a tremendous amount of research that simply needed consolidation and packaging into a simple (but not easy) framework, with sales, I knew I needed to book a first class ticket on the School-of-Hard-Knocks Express, get out there and build my business through trial, tribulation, blood, sweat, and a copious amounts of tears (and boy oh boy, there were a ton of those!)

In many ways, my first two years of business were an absolute nightmare because I was a walking trial-and-error case study. I can say with confidence that I earned an A for effort and after those first couple years of clawing and scratching to build my business, reputation and brand, I was fortunate enough to earn a smidgen of profit to reinvest into hiring a business coach who had a niche in building small business owners' revenue through better sales practices. In the short run, this was a tremendous benefit, but although it helped, after three years or so I recognized I could do better, as he was running out of things to "sell" me.

After my fifth year in business, our company's revenue started to take off in the right way (which I will explain later in regard to recurring revenue as opposed to one-time selling in the world of commissions). If you fast forward to 2024, nine years into business, I am beyond proud that we will have our first year earning at least $1 million in revenue. On top of that, my incredible wife Stephanie and yours truly will have over $1 million working for us in various investments.

As the years have progressed, I have recognized that although my career and passion is CAPitalizing people's Finances, my God-given gift of ***CAPitalizing Your Sales*** is equally, if not more, important, as it was this framework that blessed my family with the launching pad that allowed me to reinvest into myself and provide my first framework (as well as this one) to all of you. My sense is that those of you who purchased this book are, let's be frank, wanting to make more money (in some cases, significantly more money) than you are currently making. Another valuable tool I have gained through my career is that, although money is fantastic, there comes a point where you must realize that it's one thing to make money; it's another to learn to be a steward of your hard-earned success. Once you understand that, you will realize why you are TRULY reading this book in the first place, which is to ultimately gain the freedom of time. This is THE most valuable currency there is and all your mastering of sales will get you is the ability to build up yourself monetarily, which will gain you YEARS of your new-found lively freedom. All I know is that I wish I had this framework at the start of my career, as it would have easily cut my financial success growth rate from nine years down to one year, if not sooner.

It's tough for me to call myself (or anyone) an expert in any particular field because when that happens, one cannot stop ego from creeping in. Once that happens, you will be humbled. Because of that, I'd like to say that you will be a perpetual student of the sales game, as this journey is a lifelong pursuit of learning (just like anything else worth fighting for). I will also get this out of the way: don't strive for perfection. Strive for excellence. There is a zero percent chance you will be perfect in this or any framework you set your mind to, so don't prepare yourself for the letdown of falling short of perfection (take it from me, I was there!). Instead, if you strive for excellence in this process, you will be, from both a quantifiable and qualifiable perspective, at peace with your perpetual improvement. With that, it's now worth revealing approximate revenue numbers on how my business has grown from the time I started out from my apartment through the present day.

Here is proof in the pudding of *CAPitalizing Your Sales*: The All-In-One 17-step Sales Framework that saves you from ever struggling again and teaches you how to sell with sincerity. My business revenue is as follows:

- 2015: -$20,000 (welcome to starting a business!)
- 2016: $262,000
- 2017: $312,000
- 2018: $482,000
- 2019: $747,000
- 2020: $500,000
- 2021: $550,000
- 2022: $614,000
- 2023: $840,000
- 2024: $1,000,000

I want to positively caution you: your mindset is going to change for the better. As you become the best salesman or woman you know, your mindset is going to evolve from:

1. Being excited to double your income to
2. Seeing the results of your use of the *CAPitalize Your Sales Framework* and wanting more to
3. Earning so much money you won't know what to do with it (which is where CAPitalizing Your Finances comes into play) to
4. Realizing this whole framework has nothing to do with the money (*wait, what?* Talk about a teaser!) to
5. Giving back to your community, friends, family, employees (if you run a business), or a non-profit you are passionate about, and creating a legacy of prudent, honest, heartfelt and sincere salesmanship.

Now that you know a little bit about who I am and what I am about, it is time to turn the corner (or in your case...the literal page), to seeing what this book will accomplish and who it is for (Spoiler: this book is NOT for everyone...only those who wish to improve their salesmanship and their lives, so if that is not you, that's fine! I just saved you a couple hours, but unfortunately cost you hundreds of thousands of dollars... if not millions).

WHAT THIS BOOK WILL ACCOMPLISH AND WHO IT IS FOR

Let's cut to the chase! This is what you will get after reading this book.

What you will gain:
- The understanding of how to master the art of sincere networking.

- Learning keys for getting anyone into your business to learn what you do.
  - Once they are in your "office" or place of work, HOW to educate them on what you do (and by doing so, get referrals immediately).
  - Once you get a referral or prospect into your door, how to set the initial meeting stage to get them already knowing you are what they need (and how to close the sale!!!)
- Once you have a client (hopefully more than one after a while), how to keep them coming back for more (and continue to compound the referral train to their family and friends!)
- The ability to cultivate business partner relationships to build up an ULTAMITE referral pipeline.
- The art of climbing up market for larger sales and clients.
- The knowledge of how to approach online sales and social media.
- The ability to recognize the pivotal moment when you need to pivot from "external: sales to focusing on "internal" sales.

Now that you know what you will gain, this is who **CAPitalize Your Sales** is for.

1. Entry-level sales professionals between 18-29 desperately wanting to double their income.
2. Business owners with revenue under $1 million who are striving for their first million-dollar year to join the "$1,000,000 CAPitalize Club."

Now…if you are in sales and above this age group, does that mean you're disqualified from reading this book? Absolutely…I'm kidding! OF COURSE NOT! All I know is that I wrote this book with the intention of taking myself back to the moment when I started in business, which happened to be in that age range. We have coached people in sales divisions in companies well into their thirties, forties, fifties, and beyond! Remember: you are always the student of the game, never the master.

Does this also mean that if you're a business owner making over $1 million a year that you are 'too good' for this read? Quite the contrary. In fact, I could make an argument that it would be worth even more of your time on an absolute basis. Think about it: if someone reading this has a business making $500,000 a year and doubles their income, their revenue is now $1,000,000. If you are already making $1 million and you double your income, congratulations: your new revenue is $2 million. Translation: it's worth twice as much as your counterpart making $500,000. Ahhh the beauty of compounding!

Before I go on a tangent about the value of compounding that you don't want to read about due to your current (hypothetical) impatient demeanor, it's time to dive into the first chapter of our framework: *What is Your Purpose?*

Chapter 1:
What is Your Purpose?

When it comes to sales, people too often focus on the quantitative side of things, which makes sense because...let's face it...you bought this book because you want to make more money. It should be stated that there is absolutely nothing wrong with that! Where the issue lies is further down the road and much more profound, and if you are not careful, it can ruin you. Let me explain my own journey.

Now that you know what the revenue numbers were for my business from 2015 through 2024, what you clearly see is that the numbers are headed in the right direction! What you don't see is when happiness peaked in terms of financial gain. You are probably trying to guess when that actually was and the answer may shock you. One hint I will give you is that I was *definitely* happier in 2016 as opposed to 2015, as it turns out that going from losing -$20,000 to revenue of $260,000 is quite the leap. This, however, is not when I gained my sincere happiness. You're probably assuming it was 2019 before my practice (on the surface) pulled back in revenue...wrong again. *"Ok, ok... of course it's this year with the $1,000,000 mark,"* is another understandable conclusion, but you'd be wrong again.

The first thing I want to mention is that it had nothing to do with the revenue I made in any particular year (but again...not 2015). The year was 2021, which from a numbers perspective, didn't really jump off the page as earth-shattering in comparison to other years. From a technical standpoint, this is where I began to understand the business aspect of what I do in a much more comprehensive way, but from a *purpose* standpoint, this is the year where everything qualitatively clicked.

Here lies the issue all of you will have if you decide to skip over this step: there will never be enough. If all you are choosing to do is chase a number, here's a news flash: you're setting yourself up for failure. Being a competitive salesman, I'd be lying to you if I said I don't try to improve my revenue every single year. I want to be crystal clear in saying that having these goals annually and milestones throughout your career is going to be paramount to your success, but if you don't have something to fall back on that guides you to *why* you are doing this in the first place, you will succumb to the curse that I fell prey to for the first six years of my career. Part of this stemmed from the initial years of business and the fear of failure, but the primary reason why I chased a surface-level number was more due to the fact that I had zero purpose to fall back on.

Before we dive into the heavy-hitting strategies the ***CAPitalize Your Sales Framework*** provides, your first step is going to be mission critical in the grand scheme of things:

1. Set the timer for an hour.
2. Silence your phones, watches or any device that will distract you.
3. Sit with your thoughts.
4. Write everything that is important to you.
5. At the end, come up with a single sentence that will guide you for the rest of your life.

No pressure, right? It's only a single sentence that will dictate your entire future existence...relaaax! If you haven't figured it out yet, I like to joke around with the serious stuff in life. After all, life is too serious to begin with, so let's have a bit more fun with it, shall we?! Back to pseudo-serious Chris: this sentence does not have to be set in stone because you will change over time, which means your purpose will evolve. To give you some assistance, I want to share with you what I discovered my purpose was (and still is), as well as Stephanie and my family's purpose. This also brings up a quick point: it's valuable to know what your purpose is, and it can be something totally different from your family's purpose. I think of the analogy of oxygen masks on airplanes: put yours on before you assist others. If you don't know what your purpose is, how in the world are you going to help your family with theirs?!

When I first took the time to go through this exercise, I didn't take an hour...I actually took a day. I am well aware that this is a bit extreme, so an hour will get you to where you need to be, but there is nothing in the rule book that says you have to limit yourself to that. We live in a world that is tremendously attention grabbing, and I remember reading once that it takes up to twenty minutes for your mental concentration to achieve its optimal focus. This can also be lost in a second if you're distracted, so by sitting with your thoughts, you can come to terms with things in a much deeper way as opposed to being distracted 24/7. As a side note, this is a good practice to implement all together: try being with yourself for an hour without any distractions. If you can't be with yourself for an hour, ask yourself why anyone else would want to do the same with you...both *ouch* and *you're welcome*.

After going through this process, I am proud to say that my purpose is:

> To grow myself in all aspects of my life so that I can not only be a steward to my character, but instill the same mindset in those that aspire to be great.

If it is just you, perfect! If you are married and/or have kids, take care of someone in your household, etc., obviously both/all of you sitting silently in a room is *not* going to move your needle in understanding your collective purpose, but instead of sitting awkwardly for that period of time, take the hour to write down exactly what is most important to you in your family. This may take more than an hour, and that's okay! Generally speaking, the longer something takes to complete, the more fulfilled one will feel. When Stephanie and I went through our process, we discovered our family's purpose is:

> To continuously communicate with each other to further our growth as a family, which, in turn, will allow our family to assist the growth in our immediate community.

What's the point of all of this? The whole idea of this exercise is making sure you understand not only where your purpose is leading you; on top of that, once you get to a level of financial success, you still have plenty to improve on and it's no longer about "that extra dollar." If you stick to this framework, I have zero doubt that you could easily make hundreds of thousands and eventually millions of dollars. Once you get to that point, unless you are constantly trying to keep up with the Joneses, you will realize that there is much more to it than money: the game becomes all about *stewardship*.

One of the blessings of my podcast is that I have been fortunate to interview amazing people from all walks of life. As I was thinking about this chapter, the one guest that stuck out was one of my favorite authors, past guests, and friends, Gautam Baid. Gautam wrote arguably one of the greatest finance books I have ever read, *The Joys of Compounding*.[1] He states this analogy much more elegantly than yours truly, but for those of you who are not going to drop what you are doing to buy my friend's book due to your obsessive concentration and focus into *this* award-winning read, I will sum up what he calls the four pillars of wealth:

1. The first pillar is where we all start: everyone is hustling to try to make it work and get by.
2. The second pillar is when we graduate to living paycheck to paycheck, which is deemed a good thing because you are not going backwards.
3. The third pillar is where most people peak (which is totally fine as a side note) and this is what he calls the

"traditional retirement" route. People have worked hard, saved all their lives, and eventually retired off their hard-earned savings.
4. The fourth pillar is where it gets interesting. This is where few have gone. When you reach the point where you and your family are taken care of, your family's family is taken care of, you could triple/quadruple/etc. your income and your money will simply not go backwards due to the combination of amount, living within means, and investment compounding in the positive trajectory, something magical happens: You see the world for what it really is.

I tell you this because my goal is for all of you reading this to hit the fourth pillar. More likely than not, most of you are at pillar one, two, or somewhere in between. If that's the case, all you are focused on (and will be for the near future...understandably so) is turning that corner financially. By practicing the construction of your purpose, regardless of where you are, you now have the ability to mentally position yourself as if you have earned the top spot of the fourth pillar.

To say it another way, now you can enjoy the ride from a qualitative standpoint and the quantitative standpoint will take care of itself.

You're welcome.

Now that you have laid the groundwork for *why* you are going to be selling lights-out, before we dive into the techniques you are going to want to use in the world of networking events, "cold" calling, what I call "Out and About" selling and sales on social media, you are first going to be laying the foundation for getting people into your "office."

SECTION 1:
Get them into your "Office"

For those who are struggling to figure out what this first section of the book is all about, I will save you the headache: it's about getting people into your office. Sarcasm aside, this could mean your literal office, warehouse, job site, i.e., any place of work where you bring home the bacon for yourself and your family (if you have one and are the primary breadwinner). In all of my years of coaching clients, friends, and fans on catapulting their sales numbers, the forgotten topic of discussion is how to get people through your doors.

When most people think about sales and getting people into their place of work to close new business and ring the register, they immediately jump to the "acquire as many new clients as possible" category, but this is a mistake I made early on that I wish I could have gone back and had a serious do-over. By definition, if you don't have a clue how to get people onto your home turf, how in the world are you going to close *anyone*?

In this section, I am going to break down the four major hunting grounds for you to move your needle into placing potential customers and clients in your literal or metaphorical sights:

1. Networking Events
2. "Cold" Calling (this ties into networking events)
3. What I call "Out-and-About" Selling
4. Social Media Sales

In the beginning of my career, I knew that these were extremely valuable; however, like any young, hungry, and innocently distracted salesman, I was distracted by just about every other aspect of attempting to build my business. Later on in this book, you will get to learn about the advanced sales strategies of creating strategic alliances with business partners that can refer you more sales opportunities (we call those "Centers of Influence"), but these four key areas of potential sales opportunity are going to be where you truly cut your teeth in developing an award-winning foundation for becoming the best sales strategist you know.

It's also worth noting why I ordered these in this order of importance. We live in a world where face-to-face interaction means different things, whether it be in person networking events, group Zoom calls, or even community chats and blogs. When it comes down to it, there is nothing more valuable than face to face. I could make the argument that today, more than ever, meeting people in person at networking events is infinitely more value than hopping on a video call. We live in a world where things are easier than ever before, which is fine in many regards, but NOT in the avenue of, "showing how committed you are and how much you care." Think about it: how committed are you if you jump on a video call? All things being equal, not nearly as committed as when you take time to look presentable, hop in your car, head out to a networking event, and look people in the eye. Whether it's conscious or subconscious, both you and whoever you are speaking to at these events become that much closer. Remember: the more genuine the connection, the closer you are to the sale (emphasis on *genuine*, which we will get to later on).

Once you master the art of the networking event, you will get a detailed framework in the art of "Cold" Calling. Even though the technical term is cold calling, I'd prefer to call it lukewarm calling because if you play your cards right at these networking events, you will never have to truly cold call again. This is another mistake I made early on in my career, but I will save those failures for the actual chapter...I can't give away too much in the introductory section...what type of salesman would I be if I showed my entire deck of cards without any suspense to keep you coming back for more?! Technically, you *could* jump to the "Cold" Calling Chapter, but that takes all the fun out of things, plus I know you are following this framework to a T and won't do that...right...? I digress!

After you learn these first two strategies, I can't guarantee this...but I am going to CONFIDENTIALLY assume the sales bug is going to bite you so hard that you will want to sell to anyone or anything that breathes. I say this because this is when you can continue to get your reps in with what I call, "Out-and-About" selling. Not to get too far ahead in your successful career, but eventually, as you grow your business, brand, and niche, you will learn you cannot (and should not) attempt to help and close everyone. Unfortunately, when you are just starting off, despite what all the "sales gurus" say about, *"find your niche and stick to it forever and don't waver,"* you will learn in about +/- .0003 seconds that this (seemingly) sound advice goes straight out the window. Once the sales bug bites you, you will want to practice, practice, practice. The whole niche concept will sort itself out later on. Another thought to chew on: according to Indeed.com, a Bureau of Labor and Statistics survey showed that:

- From ages 18-24, people change jobs an average of 5.7 times.
- From ages 25-34, people change jobs an average of 2.4 times.
- From ages 35-44, people change jobs an average of 2.9 times.
- From ages 45-52, people change jobs an average of 1.9 times.[2]

This is all the more reason to, at the beginning, practice selling what you can to anyone with a pulse because those repetitions will become immensely more valuable when (statistically speaking) you switch jobs throughout your career. If you start out with a niche and then change your job 12.9 times according to this (staggering) statistic, you are going to struggle mightily due to having zero foundation in multi-dimensional salesmanship. If you can sell anything to anyone, the niche will become just another sale in your framework.

The last chapter in this section is about the world of social media sales. A common misconception people have with social media sales is that you can simply "throw as much on the wall as you can and see what sticks," or in other words, it's all about volume. I remember talking with my brother a few years back when we were both in the thick of things growing our respective businesses. In the world of social media management, sure, it's a completely different game than financial planning and comprehensive wealth management. However, this didn't take away from the shock I had when he said he, "sent out a couple hundred emails" to potential prospects. By no means am I knocking my brother (and even if I do, he knows it's out of genuine brotherly love); what I am saying is that there is a zero percent chance that those couple *hundred* emails to possible prospects were 100% customized for each and every company. I will take it a step further and say that *if* these businesses decided to take my brother up on his offer, unless there is some serious CAPitalizing of his Sales process, he could just as easily lose those clients. Here's the thing: in life, if something takes no time at all to gain, you can lose it just as fast. On the other hand, if someone earns a sale or recurring business after relentless, genuine connection with whoever you are coordinating with to ring your register, that person will stick with you through thick and thin. Remember this: you are not a transaction; you're a partner. Not to go off on too far of a tangent and get ahead of myself, know that there are three types of people in this world:

1. Those that have poor mindsets.
2. Those that have rich mindsets.
3. Those that have wealthy mindsets.

Poor-mindset people couldn't care less about their business relationship with you, only about the lowest cost and thinking of your purely as a transaction. This is the classic, "Screw you, what's in it for me now and always," mentality. Rich mindsets are ruthless and cutthroat in pursuing greatness at the cost of all else. Think of these people as the Poor-mindset people, only with the understanding that it takes money to make money (but again... they don't want to spend hardly anything for everything you can and will provide them). It's the wealthy mindsets that you are after and strive to emulate. These people focus on the relationship first and foremost. Obviously, cost is important, but they understand the concept of "price is what you pay, value is what you get." They understand the sincere meaning of business and want to get to know the person behind the profession. They want to be there for you and with you through thick and thin, as you would do for them in a heartbeat due to the understanding of genuine and sincere sales practices you have embedded within yourself. These are the people who would call to wish you a happy birthday, congratulate you on your big win, or take you out to lunch to simply cherish your professional relationship and expect nothing in return. THESE are the people you want to surround yourself with, both in business and in the grand scheme of life.

That tangent is critical to the world of social media reachouts because in the world of quantity, if you keep throwing everything on the wall, what sticks will be lackluster at best. In the chapter on social media sales, I will teach you the art of genuine connection (which, yes, is possible in the digital world!).

Now that you know the lay of the land for this section, let's get into the fun stuff. Let's start by ***CAPitalizing*** on Networking Events!

Chapter 2:
CAPitalize on Networking Events

When you are starting out in your business or career, there is one asset that you have that your competition does not: time. You have all the time in the world and if you recall the old saying "the most valuable currency there is time," you know that spending that time wisely is the name of the game. Especially when you start out, you know that you have no clients, no business partners, now brand...nothin.' Since this is the case for +/- 100% of people in this situation, it's best to get out there...like *right* now!

    I made a ton of mistakes early on in my career (which we will dive into throughout the book), but this is one of the major areas that I can say with confidence I absolutely nailed. After my licenses transitioned from the big firm I was previously with (which, side note...is about as quick as watching paint dry), it's safe to say I was READY to get out there and I felt like a bull in a rodeo cage. My metaphorical hooves were digging into the dirt and I could not wait for that gate of being let free to finally open. Unlike a bull, however, I needed to be extremely prudent with my time and what better way to do so than to go to every networking event I could find.

Before we continue into my journey of actually getting in the door and maximizing efficiency of the art of networking, it's worth noting an article I read about three months into my commencement of my business. As optimistic as I am, let me be incredibly blunt: the first few years of sales will be both the best and worst time of your life all at once. The days are long and after the honeymoon phase wears off and life gets REAL, there will be moments where you will doubt yourself (it happens to all of us). I say this because three months into my journey, I had that exact feeling and it's NOT fun. Looking for answers, I turned to none other than Mr. Google and came across an article by one of the financial planning personalities, Michael Kitces, on building a financial planning business. Even though he specializes in company analysis within my profession, this article saved me and would save anyone who reads it. Fortunately/unfortunately, Mr. Kitces tends to be a little long-in-the-tooth when it comes to explanation, so I will summarize the article in four easy bullet points:

1. Year 1 – Do business with anyone you can.
2. Year 2 – Repeat year 1, just keep grinding.
3. Year 3 – Still grinding, but now people from years 1 and 2 are referring you.
4. Year 4 – shifting from grinding out business to fielding referrals as business starts to come in!

To say it another way:

1. Year 1 – Become Known
2. Year 2 – Become Liked
3. Year 3 – Become Trusted
4. Year 4 – Game Over[3]

Before we get back to the networking event mastery, write this somewhere where you can remind yourself of this every single day. Your morale and eventual success will thank you.

When I was finally able to let loose and get out there to make a name for myself, acting out of prudency (but adrenaline filled, so still sprinkled with instinct), the first thing I did was look up my local Chamber of Commerce networking calendars. I already had ordered my business cards, letterhead, and all the needed marketing things to legitimize myself, so now I needed an easy place to go to practice my salesmanship, meet as many people as possible, and continue to utilize that invaluable currency of time that I had (at the time) a TON of in my back pocket. In my community, there are three or four prominent Chamber of Commerce groups, so I made sure to head over to their websites, mark off every networking event for the year ,and not miss one: ever. I knew that if I was going to become known, I needed to become KNOWN, a.k.a. be everywhere all the time. That would only hasten my known-to-liked-to-trusted track.

The second place I looked into was the local Rotary and I made sure to do the exact same thing. Similar to any Chamber of Commerce type organization, Rotary groups are a wonderful place to get to know your local community (and for them to know you). One thing I noticed was these two organizations seldom if ever had events at the same time, so I quickly concluded that these two would help me make sure my time went from plentiful to strategically limited.

One thing I did *not* do early on that I wish I did was look up nonprofits or local businesses I aligned with that regularly threw fun events, as I would have hopped on those as well. It can be pseudo-taboo to go to these types of events to shoot your shot; however, I have a different take on it (obviously, or else I wouldn't be writing this in the first place...but I digress). You're human. Whoever you are talking to is human. It's human nature to get to know people at these types of events and if someone asks what you do, own it and be genuine!

Later in the book, we will talk about business partners, strategic alliances, centers of influence and high-level ways to rev your sales' success, but for now, your main goal is to litter your schedule with as many networking events as possible. For those of you who run your own business, you have a massive advantage because you own your time. The obvious disadvantage is that your revenue depends solely on you ringing your register, so in the short run, I can tell you from firsthand experience the discomfort will be felt...*a lot*. In the long run; however, your bank account will thank you (or thank me...you get my point.) For those in a sales position with your employer, one thing you don't necessarily have is the flexibility in your schedule; however, in many ways, that is a huge benefit because most sales positions have built-in referral opportunities coming through the doors throughout the day (think of a car dealership as an easy example). One common criticism I hear from people in this situation is that once they leave their respective place of work, their job is done for the day. Let me tell you something: the most successful salesmen, saleswomen, and business owners out there *never stop selling*. Let's say you are a car salesman. I get it: the days at the dealership are LONG and often you aren't out of there until most of the networking events are done, so you couldn't make it even if you tried. My question is this: what's stopping you from going to these events on your days off? Someday when your brand or business is crushing it, you will have those days to truly unplug and recharge, but I can tell you that in the first two years of my business, time off was never a thought. Even today, I sincerely struggle to unplug and have to force myself to do so (ask my better half or amazing employee if you think I'm exaggerating). If you want to be the best and truly **CAPitalize Your Sales**, know that those days will come, but they aren't here now.

Once I got to those events, I made a mental note to make the event a game. My goal was to meet as many people and collect as many business cards as I could. In this particular area, that was not a problem for me, but there was a gigantic mistake I wish I corrected early on:

I made the conversations about me.

Even if I was genuinely curious about the person I was talking to, in the back of my mind (who am I kidding...it was in many cases smacked across my forehead!), the ONLY thought on my mind was, "How can I get this person to become a client?" In the old Chris's defense, if the business wasn't closed, food was not in the cards. Even with that being said, if I had known what I am about to tell you, I could have both alleviated that selfish thought AND rung my register exponentially faster and more often.

When you approach someone at these events, obviously introduce yourself and ask what they do, but once the pleasantries are (quickly) complete, here comes the secret: make it your mission to tell as little about you as possible for as long as possible in the conversation.

Wait...what?

I know what you're thinking: how in the world will this ring YOUR register? Think about this for a second: who is the best salesman or saleswoman you know? Once you think of whoever it is, what made them so great? One of the main bullet points I can say with near certainty: they hardly talked about themselves and you felt heard from start to finish.

You see, people want to talk about themselves. Even introverts, to an extent, want to share something about themselves. It's human nature. If you have a newborn, you cannot help but want to scream about it from the mountaintops (for better or worse in the case of sleep deprivation). If you just started a new business or a position at your dream job, you want to tell people about it as a thing of pride. Specific to business and sales (here's the kicker), if you are at one of these events, the chances are you are like- minded with them in the fact that they are trying their best to get the word out and would absolutely die to have someone help them succeed (and they'll never forget it either).

Bingo.

Once the pleasantries are complete, I would ask a couple variations of a 'sincere starter' type of question:

1. What is/are some of the most exciting thing(s) you are working on right now?
2. What are the greatest challenges you think you'll face (or are facing) in the near future?
3. Who do you know at this event? Were they the ones that inspired you to come out or was there another reason and what was it?
4. Tell me more about what you do, as I am intrigued by your line of work and want to know more about it, as I may need someone like you in the near future (or have clients that may need someone like you in the near future).

Did you catch what these questions did? For starters, they do NOT require a yes or no answer. Open-ended questions are the gift that keeps on giving and there's a key reason: when you ask an open-ended question, you are essentially asking whoever you are talking to, *"What can I do to genuinely get to know you as well as earn a genuine sale in the process?"* Here lies the key, as the greatest salesmen and saleswomen know:

The more genuine you are, the greater your success will be.

Your goal when you meet with EVERY person at these events is to:

1. Figure out everything about their line of work.

2. *Genuinely* discover what their greatest pain points are and take a mental note.
3. Get them into your office or place of work to continue that conversation, further your discovery, introduce them to the right connections to better their business after the meeting and, during that chat, ask if it would be all right if you could educate them on what you do (note how it's NOT about selling...you are always educating).

Back when I was starting, I made a grave mistake: I would tell whoever I was talking to that I would call them the following day to get something on the calendar...there is SO much that is wrong with this. First, how in the world would I have known what on God's green earth they would be doing in the morning? What if this was their busiest time of the week? What if they were in their busiest time of year? What if they had an appointment with a doctor? The list goes on and on, but I wasted HUNDREDS of hours by doing this. Know this: until the sale (both direct and indirect) has been made, ALWAYS get them on the calendar for the next meeting.

Once you have built that connection with whomever you are talking to and got their business card and contact information in your phone, keep your phone out and pull up your calendar to lock them into the books! This is more of an art than a science and I tend to make anything stressful humorous (if you haven't figured that out yet) and so I would say something like this.

"So here's the deal: as award-winning a conversation as this has been, unless we put something on the calendar, you'll never be

able to tell me how I can further help you, so could you take the three seconds to take out your phone, open your calendar and let's get something down, as I mean it when I say that I genuinely want to help you out."

I'm not exaggerating when I say that, in my experience, roughly 70-75% of those you are talking to won't even hesitate to take out their phones and get something on the books. You send the calendar invite to them, make sure they got it, let them know that you will call the day before to confirm they are still on for getting together, and then excuse yourself to repeat until the event is over.

That last part I mentioned was the key I was missing for YEARS and it could have saved me at least the years in terms of compounding my financial success. This is where it gets to be incredible: the more genuinely interested you are in those that you are talking with (as well as interested in helping them by introducing them to whomever they need the most), the faster your business will grow. Let me explain.

In the world of investment analysis, there are three financial statements companies live or die by:

1. Balance Sheet (what it's worth)
2. Income Statement or Profit-&-Loss Statement (how much it makes)
3. Cash Flow Statement (where the income is coming from)

In the Balance Sheet, there is a line item titled "Goodwill," and the technical accounting definition is the difference between what something is worth and what someone is willing to pay for it. It's extremely abstract, but the most valuable companies in the world have the greatest Goodwill. In some ways, you could think of it as the value of one's brand. In that case, it is the most valuable asset a business has and it takes *years* to build, but once built, it's extremely difficult to lose and the power of compounding continues to skyrocket it's financial success.

> By committing to your act of networking, you are building your greatest asset of all: your goodwill (or character).

Trust me when I say that the more interactions you have practicing this method, the more business opportunities will naturally flow to you at these events. I remember back in 2019, I met one of my largest clients at a networking event through an introduction from a connection I made four years ago where I simply gave my connection exactly what I laid out to you. That new client has referred my business a tremendous amount of opportunity and it all goes back to genuine curiosity.

Before we dive into CAPitalizing on "Cold Calling" (off of the networking event), I want to leave you with an award-winning nugget I was fortunate to learn early on: don't try to fight a fight you are going to lose. If you are starting off, what does your competition have that you don't?

- Brand recognition
- Money and resources
- Marketing techniques
- Research and development capabilities
- Staff depth

The list goes on and on, but here's the sole advantage you have that trumps anything your competition throws at you: your ability to go from a total stranger to QUICKLY becoming a trusted business partner who *genuinely* wants to help whoever you are speaking with in any way possible. A major company can never give you that.

Chapter 3:

CAPitalize on "Cold" Calling (off the networking event)

If you remember the last chapter, you will recall that at these mission-critical networking events, it is crucial that, right before you part ways with your new-found (possible) business partners, you get them on the calendar. In a perfect world, if you play your cards right, you wouldn't even need to master the "cold" calling technique I am about to lay out; however, you will *quickly* discover that the world is far from perfect, *especially* in sales. God works in interesting ways (which are mysterious to you and me) and I am blessed that I messed up the art of getting people on the calendar early in my career because it led me to this new skill you are about to acquire. I also want to note that this skill will become extremely handy as you start to move up market in your sales career, as I have gained some of my greatest business partners, clients, and even friends by using these tools which are about to be at your fingertips.

Let's start where we left off: the day after the networking event. You have all of these business cards and contacts in the palm of your hand...now what?! Remember you have one goal when you are starting out in the world of sales: FILL THAT SCHEDULE! The day after these events, I would call *every* contact I gained information from the evening prior and the best part was that, since it hadn't been twenty-four hours (on top of the fact that I *always* told them I would give them a call the following day), it was never a surprise to them, and that alone gives you yet another leg up in getting closer to ringing the register.

The general flow of the call went something like this:

New-found Business Partner: "Hello, this is XYZ."

Me: "XYZ! This is Chris Panagiotu, your new-found friend you met at (name of event) last night. I wanted to stay true to my word and since I promised to call you in the morning, here I am keeping that promise! I sincerely appreciated our conversation last night and wanted to continue it, as I want to learn more about you and see how I can send business your way."

I would follow this up with:

1. "Is now a good time to take a few seconds and align our calendars to get something on the books?" or,
2. "What days and times of day work best for you?" or,
3. If they are busy or you can tell they are busy: "When would be a great time for me to call you back and put something on

the calendar? As you and I both know, if it doesn't get onto our calendars, it won't happen and I do not want to break my promise with you or myself, as my word is everything."

If you are reading this and thinking to yourself, "Geez, this feels super salesy," that's because it is...and that should make you feel fantastic. You should always remind yourself that because you are genuinely trying to serve whoever you are speaking to, the sale (whether direct or indirect) is going to better that person's life in the best way imaginable. So the sale is not just to pad your pockets; it's to sincerely improve that person's life. Reread this section again with the correct lenses and you will immediately realize the power of genuine salesmanship. This also reiterates the importance of making sure whoever you are talking to is always scheduled on the calendar until the sale is complete. If whatever you are providing is that important to the person you are talking to (or referrals they could send your way), you will stop at nothing until you better your new-found friend's situation.

As you have probably discovered, this is not the traditional cold calling of the past. I am fortunate that I haven't had to dive into that world. In my profession as a Certified Financial Planner, there is a "Do Not Call" list. If you do call someone on that list, you could be in serious trouble, so I was forced to find ways to get creative without direct cold calling. With my business, the majority of what I do is personal financial planning for accredited families[4]; however, one niche I carved out for myself early on was constructing and overseeing company retirement plans. Fast forward to today and it's been an incredible value-add for my clients that run businesses, as it's another layer I can provide that most in my industry either can't or simply won't touch (frankly... due to laziness). However, when I started out, I was no different than you, a.k.a. no clients. I mention this because I quickly discovered that even though I could not call people on the DNC list, there was no rule in my industry that said I couldn't call a business to peek at helping them with their retirement plan. This is key because, if you go back to the networking events, these are all hosted by *someone or some company*. Because of this fact, I would investigate the host's retirement plan and, if they had one, gather some intel on their situation. If they didn't have one, I had an arrow to pull from my quiver. (It's worth noting that this fact is regularly accessible online, so by no means am I some top-level detective!) Once I got to the event, I would quickly scan the list of the owner or key employee running the event. I would use the same technique I mentioned above, with a slight twist. Because I knew a sale was (in one way or another) starring me in the face, I would promise them I would call and the next day go through the same steps with one key difference: I would ask them what they are doing for their company's retirement plan. By no means was I trying to close them right then and there; I was simply asking. If they said they were not doing anything and don't even have a plan, I would ask what has held them back from pursuing one. I would keep asking and asking and asking until, after I got them on the calendar to go to their office and learn more about their business, I would dangle the carrot to get them intrigued by what I could offer. I would say something like this:

> *I want this conversation to be about me learning as much about your business as possible, but for what it's worth, because you*

mentioned (XYZ needs) that I coincidentally happen to fill, if we have time towards the end of our conversation, it could be helpful to hear my two cents, as it's kinda/sorta my career and life purpose, but alrighty, I will see you on (day) at (time) and cannot wait to learn more about you, (new business partner's name)!

Notice how I slipped it in there, sprinkled in some humor and immediately moved back to the primary task at hand: helping them. It's also keeping in line with your genuine interest in them. Remember: people will remember who genuinely helped them and only for the better. If you hard sell them, they will remember, but the short-term gain of the sale is a long-term pain in a tarnished reputation.

The last part of the "Cold" call is a slight change to what you just read. Let's say you did your homework, but were simply not able to connect with any of the hosts at the event for whatever reason. You still want to meet with them and could see value in partnering in some way, but up until this point, you're stuck. Technically...that's not true. You just need to alter what you just learned! Let's say you call and the front desk picks up. I would say something like this (after pleasantries):

My name is Chris Panagiotu and I was at your company's networking event last night and wanted to connect with (Owner, CFO, i.e., key employee) and was bombarded with conversations and couldn't connect with them. I actually was wondering if I could connect with them to see if I could get something on the calendar, as I could use what your company provides and value personal connection with those I do business with.

I would follow up with either:

1. *Do you know who would be able to get something on the calendar for me to come out and learn more about your business?*
2. *Would you be able to connect me or set up a time for us to chat on the phone and take it from there?*

Always, always, *always* get the next meeting on the calendar.

Before we move on to the next chapter on "Out-and-About" Selling, it's worth noting that, if you want to pursue traditional cold calling, all of the tools you just acquired still remain true. Out of all my years in business, I can think of one...*only one* person that could pull off the traditional cold-calling technique successfully, and that is simply due to all of his stars aligning with his God-given gifts of a suave voice, natural charisma, and unique charm. It's the classic "he could sell ice to an Eskimo," type of scenario and, unfortunately, 99.999% of people don't have that. Here's a little secret: for nearly anyone reading this book, there is no such thing as traditional cold calling. Even if you call someone out of the blue, make sure to do your homework and *really* understand who you are talking to before you call, because when someone answers, you better have your genuine ducks in a row, or else you're royally screwed (especially if that person spreads the word on you botching the initial reach-out).

Chapter 4:
CAPitalize on "Out-and-About" Selling

What does it mean to sell while "Out-and-About"? Up until this point, you have walked through the ins and outs of what to do (and *not* to do) in the world of networking events, following up, and landing in respective places of work to move your financial needle. Since you are reading this book, I can almost guarantee that you are madly in love with the idea of becoming massively successful in selling your craft, which means that you need more at your fingertips than simply what we spoke about in previous chapters. Think about it: you know the ins and outs of how to CAPitalize on the whole networking event process, but what happens if you see a prospective customer in the Starbucks line, in the supermarket, at a bar or, heck, even your chiropractor's office??? Now you need to add this new tool to your portfolio because if you are truly committed to your craft, you love what you do, and you *know* what you can provide will change society for the best, there is a zero percent chance you will "shut off" your salesmanship once a networking event is finished. If you are in sales in any way, shape or form, remember this: mind your ABS. What is ABS?

Always Be Selling.

Not only is minding your ABS in the physical sense a huge positive, it's also mission critical in the world of sales. If you are truly going to pursue being the best in sales, you must realize that this is a lifelong commitment and there is no turning off that metaphorical switch. From here on out, you are all in, all the time, everywhere. (Side note: the last sentence is applicable to every aspect of your life, so you're welcome for that little bonus nugget of wisdom!)

When I first started out in my business, it was a combination of loving what I do and also needing to not starve that lit *quite* the fire under my you-know-where. I could not tell you how many times I struck up conversations with people just about everywhere I went but...as you could imagine...it was more for the benefit of my financial well-being as opposed to genuinely learning to connect with whoever it was I was talking to. If I could go back and hit the redo button, I would have leaned 100% into the genuine connection, as the compounding of my positive reputation and character would have catapulted me that much faster to success. Let's look at some scenarios and get your mind thinking...and fast, because in moments like this, you've got about three seconds to make something happen (and continue to happen) or let the opportunity evaporate in front of your very eyes. I can tell you with certainty that the feeling of, *"If only I'd said something"* is the absolute worst feeling in the world.

Let's pretend you are in a Starbucks line since that was one of the first hypothetical examples I mentioned. The man in front of you looks like a great guy to strike up a conversation with for whatever reason (dressed well and put together, on the phone having what appears to be a high-level conversation, etc.). You want to say something, but you don't know where to begin. If you have ever been in this situation, you are not alone, as I personally have been there too many times to count! The first thing that I would analyze is what is this guy's deal.

Now...if you read this last sentence like, *"What the heck is up with this guy?!"* that was <u>not</u> where I wanted to go with that (although it is admittedly pretty funny and we've also all been there too). What I mean is what is going on with him. Some examples that come to mind:

- What's in his hands? Pad, paper, pencil? If so, what's he writing about? Does he seem far along in the process?
- Is he wearing a watch? If so, what type is it? If it's a nice brand, what's the story behind his purchase? Did he get it as a gift? Is he a collector and that's what makes him tick? (Unintentional pun, but have to give myself credit here).
- If he's wearing glasses, what brand are they? Where did he go or does he go to get his eyes tested? What made him choose this particular pair and what has been his experience with this pair in comparison to others?

I could go on and on, but do you see what I am doing here? This is mission critical because simply by appearing, you could gather a minimum of...I don't know...twenty or thirty conversation starters. Here's the dealbreaker though: if you come off as asking just to make a business move, even the most clueless human can see right through that. I cannot tell you how many times this has happened to me. I can vividly recall in our old office space right before we moved out, the property manager came in and had the awkward 1.5 seconds between saying hi to me and then following up with, "How's that new baby doing?" Let's be really honest: that guy could have given two rats about my (at the time) five-month old baby girl (and I could tell he totally forgot we even had a girl, so he pivoted to the baby term—rookie mistake in the sales book, I must say). I knew this was the case because I immediately said she was fine and then he hopped right into the pitch about how my teammate and I had been amazing tenants and he'd hate to lose us blah blah blah blah blah. The dude even had the balls to ask if he needed a commercial broker at the end of the chat just to wring the last dollar out of us on the way out.

I could very well be wrong about what happened, and he could have been well-intentioned and just had one hell of an off day in the sales department, but because you don't get second chances in life, perception is reality. Think about if he walked in and asked, "How is that baby girl of yours doing? I can't remember exactly...what is she...three to four months old now?" or, "I wanted to tell you that we are super bummed at seeing ya go and I get it if you are all taken care of, but if you need any help with anything on your way out, I am here for you." Would

I have changed my mind? Nope...because I'm the type of guy that once I decide something, it's done; however, the perception would have been drastically different and that is more valuable than maintaining a couple extra dollars.

One more scenario I wanted to touch on is if you are at a familiar place and someone is talking to someone you know and you have a good feeling about them just like the guy in the hypothetical Starbucks line. An example that comes to mind is actually my chiropractor's office (I wasn't joking at that example either!). University Place Chiropractic is like family to me and I know the Doc and staff to the point where I greet myself on the phone when I call as, "Favorite Patient Chris Panagiotu" (because I am...duh!). I mention this because there have been dozens—heck, hundreds of times when I have gone there and struck up a conversation with whoever is at the front desk, another patient comes up, I include them in the conversation, and within two minutes they are asking who I am and what I do. At places like this, that you go to more often or not (for you it could be a particular grocery store, bar, etc.), with those genuine interactions, all it takes is one of those conversations with a person and *every* time after, the connection blossoms. Before you know it, they won't be able to help themselves from asking what you do because you have been so interested in them that they want to work with you in any way possible.

Out of all of the chapters in the *Get them Into Your "Office"* section, "Out-and-About" Selling is by far the most difficult and will not be your ticket to the CAPitalized promised land, so you're probably wondering why I even went over this with you in the first place. Use the sport analogy: you're getting your reps in. ***CAPitalize Your Sales*** is all about consistency and repetition. Your sales "muscle" needs to be exercised often and unlike lifting actual weights, your sales "muscle" can be worked out twenty-four hours a day, seven days a week, and 365 days a year. I cannot tell you when exactly these reps will come in handy, but I can say for myself that when I was in meetings to bring in some of my largest clients, if it wasn't for the *years* of consistent repetition I would not have had the experience to close them.

That's another bonus nugget of wisdom: in the world of sales and business, experience does not come from age; it comes from the number of meetings and interactions.

Now that you have learned about selling in the live world, I am going digital. It's time for you to learn how to CAPitalize on Social Media Sales.

Chapter 5:
CAPitalize on Social Media Sales

U p until this point in the book (as well as recent history in general), the main point of focus has been the strategies, tips, and techniques to get possible business partners or clients into your respective place of work and get that much closer to a sale while meeting face to face. In case the title of this chapter wasn't blatantly obvious enough for you, you are about to learn the mastery of sales online in the world of social media. Before we dive into that, it's worth noting that I admittedly was late to the game, as I did not have any social media presence whatsoever until year five or so in my business. Part of that was extremely intentional and the other reason was...well...you'll put two and two together.

Being a young, hungry (both for greatness and literal food), and energized twenty-three-year-year old man, for whatever reason, I had it in me to know that distractions were abundant and I needed to get rid of as many of them as possible, *immediately*.

Sure, my industry's compliance pains helped move that needle mightily, but I was also simply not interested in hopping on Facebook, X (Twitter at the time), or Instagram to see what everyone else was doing. It didn't matter and was a waste of my time, so without hesitation, social media was a no for the longest time.

Another negative to social media was (and still is today) the fact that people get so incredibly locked into their phones or computers that they forget how to genuinely communicate with people in person. That sentence alone could be an entire book topic on its own, but for the sake of *this* book, I am going to stay on topic. If I were going to remember all these people I met with in regards to their name, place of work, what made them tick, what type of person they were (which we will get into later in the book), etc., my brain did not have had the bandwidth to fill itself with anything other than sales, business, and the commitment to my craft.

It's worth noting that, before you hit the social media sales bandwagon, I would *strongly* recommend that you take a path similar to mine. There are many reasons why, but the first noteworthy reason is that, for the most part, your most genuine connections will come from those you meet in person. The easiest example for my current professional day to day is my podcast. We are incredibly fortunate to have a top-tier, professionally built-out podcast studio, and I say this because we have had a number of incredible guests fly in to do the show in person. Obviously this is not possible for every guest (whether because of cost or schedule conflicts), so video recordings are a way of life. Let me tell you something: there is absolutely **zero** contest between in person and video. The in-person guest shows get the better...well...everything ten out of ten times. The video quality is spotless, the audio isn't choppy and, most importantly, the interactions are real. I'm not saying video recordings aren't real, but there's just something about having someone in person that makes it all the better.

I am not telling you to wait five years like I did...who am I kidding...you most likely already use social media regularly! What I am saying is that, if you are already on it or are not and thinking about hopping on, give yourself six months of *not* checking it (or thinking about it). You will be blown away at how much more locked in you will be with every conversation.

With that being said...I am going to stop kicking the can down the road and assume you are past all of that (or flat out won't listen to the advice I just gave) and get into the world of digital sales.

First, you have to know your audience and possible customer inside and out, which means you need to know which social media platform they use most frequently. It's a bit different for me now that I wear several hats, but when I first began unlocking the power of social media sales, my go-to was LinkedIn due to the other professionals that I worked with or were looking to partner with. It took me a while to figure out the ins and outs of posting, liking and commenting on others' content, but what clicked for me much more rapidly was the art of the initial reach-out.

One HUGE advantage with social media is that you can tell who you and your new-found contact have in common. Personal connection trumps everything. You can also tell if they went to the same school, likes the same music, the list goes on and on. This is all key because it takes the guessing game out of the picture, so unlike that random dude in the Starbucks line from the last chapter, you already know a ton about your target. (It's both super cool and *incredibly* creepy all at the same time!). The next question is this:

Now what?

In many ways, the process of connection is similar to that of the networking event; however, there are a few key differences to consider. For one, you are connecting with someone out of the blue, so you don't know how your tone will come across in an initial connection request. You may think you sound super sincere, but they may read it as slimy and sleazy. A huge drawback is that you can't read this connection's body language, eye patterns, or verbal cues that tell you what type of person they are. So how do you make sure that, when they read the connection request, the urge to respond and connect is almost automatic?

The first thing I would do is investigate the connections you two have in common. If you believe this connection is perfect for getting your reps in, assuming you have someone in common, try something like this:

> Hi (Name)! (XYZ Platform) shot your profile page to the top of my feed multiple times over the past few days and I can see why: it turns out we have one of my all-time best buddies in common (friend in common) and anyone that is connected with (friend in common) has my seal of approval! I would love to set up a time to zoom and get to know more about you, as I want to surround myself with like-minded people. Would you be open for a Zoom on (XYZ date and time)?

What did you just do? It's simple: you genuinely reached out after doing your homework, stated honestly why you want to connect, and linked you and your future business partner to someone you already know quite well. If your possible new business partner or client does connect and wants to hop on a call or video chat, without knowing anything else about this person, I can say the odds of getting a sale skyrocketed. By the time you connect with them over a call, you will want to immediately ask them (after pleasantries, of course), how they know your common connection, tell them how you and your common connection initially met, and then jump right into asking what this person does. One of my favorite questions to ask is, *"What's your story?"* because the answer will reveal SO many avenues to a sale, they are almost endless. You always have to remind yourself to, when in doubt, ask another question. Just as you would otherwise, towards the end of the call get another meeting on the calendar if it feels as though there could be some connection going forward. Depending on how the call goes, sometimes (in fact, more often than not), they will ask you what you do, and this is where you have two options. You can either tell them (and even better yet, show them, if possible) or ask them if it is all right if you continue to learn more about them and then set up a call at the end to return the favor and show them at that time. Regardless of the outcome, one thing's for sure: you know they are interested. Whether or not you are specifically for them is irrelevant because, in one way or another, you are about to make some money.

What happens if you don't have anyone in common but you really want to connect with this person? There are a couple ways to go about it, but it's much more of an uphill battle. If you send an initial connection request and they connect, that's a start, but most people connect and forget about it. Something I did back in the day that worked wonders was, after the initial connection, I would look into their profile page, and after I learned more about them...call me crazy...I would call them. You read that right: I would actually call them! That call would go something like this:

Is this (new-found connection)? My name is Chris Panagiotu and I noticed that you recently connected with me on (social media platform) and after looking at your business, I wanted to formally call and introduce myself and see if we could set up a time for me to get to know more about your business, as my clients (and myself) might need your business's services in the future and I like to get to know the partners I work with on a personal level. Before we look into our calendars, I noticed on your page (something that is unique) and was curious, what made you get into XYZ or choose ABC?

This whole process tells your new-found business partner a TON about who you are. Not only are you serious about your connection (regardless of whether it is online or in person), you always make sure to reach out to those that you connect with, are dead set on wanting to work with *them* in some way, are committed to set aside your schedule to meet with them to learn more about what they do, AND you want to send them business if at all possible after the fact. Name me a business owner or business partner that would say no to that.

Social media sales have this perception of throwing as much on the wall as possible and see if you can make any of it stick. In reality, that will lead you to a sad, defeating track record and, just like any phony salesman or saleswoman out there, people will see right through you. I cannot tell you how many times I have been messaged on social media and in .0003 seconds, I delete the initial contact request or direct message because I know there is absolutely no genuine interest in me whatsoever. On the flip side, some of my all-time best friends have come from genuine contacts on social media and these are the people you want to have in your life because when the bad times come rolling in, they are going to vouch for you. Most people on social media are in it for themselves. By simply showing your genuine connection with others, you are going to be light years ahead of the game and, of course, that much closer to padding your pocketbooks. (If you haven't picked up one of the main themes of this book quite yet, it's genuine connection.)

Before we take the GIGANTIC next step of transitioning from outside of your place of work to inside where the sales shall most certainly occur, it's worth giving an overview of what you will need to do to make either these business partners or possible prospects lifelong clients.

Buckle up...there's a lot.

SECTION 2:

How to turn a connection into a client

Up until this point, you have learned the major strategies I learned to make sure I got as many prospects into my office as humanly possible, but the next series of chapters will teach you the ultimate step in converting possible buyers into diehard clients and/or business partners. This section is THE section I wish I had on day one when I started my business because it took me nearly six...*six* years to figure this stuff out. Getting people into the office was one thing, but actually getting paid is an entirely different skill and it separates the haves from the never-made-its.

Here is a brief overview into what you will learn over the coming chapters to *actually* ring your register:

1. You will learn about the three types of people and how to match them with their own...shall we say...selves (trust me, it'll make sense).

2. You will take a deep dive into *how* to conduct your initial meeting with prospective clients.
3. Once the prospect is on the books to come back for a presentation meeting (where you actually close the client), you will learn the play-by-play on how to conduct this meeting so that the prospective client knows that you heard their needs loud and clear.
4. After you convert your prospects into clients, you will master the art of keeping them coming back for more and more and more!

This next section is going to be, without a doubt, the most intense, as you are going to turn up your listening and analyzing skills to a whole new level. Learning the art of mirroring both one's verbal and physical cues is important, but what's more important is tracking where one's eyes travel. I remember when I was initially studying these strategies that if you combine these three techniques into one, the closing rate of bringing on new clients jumps by a staggering 38%. Unfortunately, I could not for the *life* of me find that study (trust me...I spent *hours* searching for this gem), but even if the study was exaggerating the results by double, I'd still take an improved close rate of nearly 20% any day of the week. Think about it: if you had 20 sales opportunities a week for, say, $500 per sale, if you were closing four a week, that would mean you'd earn (assuming you work 52 weeks out of the year) $104,000. If the research is off by half and your close rate was only improved by 20% (going from closing four of twenty to five of twenty), you'd now earn $130,000...who wouldn't want a raise like that?!

Not to jump too far ahead in the book, but I will be providing you a tool to make sure you keep track of first meetings, closing meetings, sales amounts, and so much more, so I am not only strongly urging you...I am ordering you ***do not jump to the end of this book to sneak a peek.*** You need to understand this all conceptually before you start diving into data tracking. I went nearly four years without tracking any data other than in my head, so don't sweat it when it comes to tracking numbers left and right. That brings up another point I wish I knew when I started this journey of ***CAPitalizing Your Sales***:

Enjoy
The
Ride

These next few chapters are going to provide you with the highest adrenaline rush of your life and you are going to be so profoundly hooked into this process that you are going to forget to enjoy every second of it. Part of it could be due to the fact that you are just starting out and, if this is the case, are most likely broke. When you have that feeling of treading water and not being able to get ahead, you are going to lock into breaking through that financial ceiling and you will stop at nothing until you get there. I was there and I know exactly what you are going through. August 2017 was hands-down the lowest point of my career, as the majority of the revenue my business brought in came in the mid-to-late fall months and that month was do or die. I had just brought on my amazing teammate (who I couldn't afford), was struggling to pay off debts, and was *clawing* to get those debts obliterated and break through to profitability. Unfortunately, I wasn't able to step back and realize those struggling hustle years were jam-packed with some of the greatest moments of my life. When I would get a potential new client on the books, I would get *beyond* hyped in my office just at the fact that I was that much closer to making it happen for myself and my future family. If you thought I was happy then, the amount of adrenaline-packed joy I earned when someone became a client was a multitude of AT LEAST ten. I am telling you all of this because during those moments, I never gave myself the opportunity to sincerely appreciate those wins and, in many ways, I would give anything to have those days and moments back so I could truly embrace them.

Now that you have the mindset I wish I had when I was at your stage in your career, it's time to get into this! Let's start by discussing the three types of people you NEED to know about, because that's going to set the stage for me painting the picture of the greatest sales process you have ever witnessed.

Chapter 6:

The three types of people you NEED to know

Up until this point, you have not had any groundbreaking technical information thrown at you. There's a reason for that: sales is not supposed to be technical. The more genuine you are, the higher your closing rate will be, which is the ultimate desired outcome. This chapter is one of the few exceptions where we hop aboard the technical bandwagon because we are going to dive into the three types of people you NEED to know (if you didn't already know that by reading the blatantly obvious chapter title). What will *not* be obvious is how you conduct yourself with each one.

You and I both know that everyone has something that makes them tick. Maybe it's sports. Sometimes it's food. Occasionally it's business. You get my point: there is one favorite topic for everyone out there and most sales coaches will guide you to quickly discover what that topic is for whoever you are talking to and lure that dopamine spike of discussing that love into a sale. Talk about disingenuous! Not to mention that it's flat-out wrong.

There are three types of people in the world of sales:

1. Visuals
2. Auditories
3. Kinesthetics

You are most likely familiar with visuals, as these people want to *see* a message or result. Auditories are a close second in terms of commonality and are more interested in how something *sounds*. Kinesthetics are the rarest of the three and are influenced the most by how they *feel* about a particular outcome.

It is mission critical that you understand these three types of people because who these people are will dictate how they process and retain the information provided to them. What's equally important is knowing how they will interact with you. It's worth noting a bit more about each one before you take a deep dive into visuals, auditories, and kinesthetics.

When it comes to interacting with visuals, these people make sense of words by constructing or recalling images in their mind. If the picture cannot be drawn in their head, it is going to be difficult for them to understand what you are saying. In the auditories department, if they cannot hear the result play out in their head, chances are it isn't going to happen. These people frequently talk to themselves internally to understand what you are saying (but not in a schizophrenic murderer sense...hopefully.) Lastly, the kinesthetic crowd (say that ten times fast... bonus points if you can do it with a lisp and not laugh) is all about feelings. You know the saying "go with your gut?" This is kinesthetics to a T. If they don't feel like you are their type of person within the first sixty seconds, you might as well walk away because they have checked out.

Before you dive into how to tackle each one, it is important to ask yourself which one you are. Go through this exercise: take a moment to think about your morning. What do you remember the most? Don't think too profoundly about this, but think quickly about what you saw, heard, and felt. If a visual memory comes to mind, you're most likely a visual. If you remember more of what you initially heard in the AM, you're probably an auditory. Lastly, if a feeling is what sticks out, kinesthetics is the name of your game.

Now that you have gone through this exercise with yourself, it's time to dive into determining what type of person each business partner or prospect is (or anyone for that matter). You will be able to figure this out with two simple points in conversation:

1. The direction of their eyes when they think.
2. The words and premise of the words they use when talking.

Let's start by diving into visuals.

VISUALS

Visuals' minds work in a...well...visual sense. Their viewpoint of the world around us is all about 3D. If there is an idea that can be *seen*, the chances are the closing rate is going to skyrocket.

Beautiful pictures and easy to see ideas are the names of the game. According to atlassian.com, research has found that 65% of the general population fit this category[5] so if you master this type of person's mentality, you are ahead of most. If you are in an industry where the sale is right in front of you (like cars, builders, gardening), it's much easier because you can show them exactly what the results have been and tailor the conversation from there. If you are in a more service-based business (CPA, attorney, life insurance), charts, graphs, and pretty scenes are going to be extremely helpful when it comes down to moving the needle in the closing direction.

Just as anyone does with anything in life, visuals will give you hints to tell you how they think. This is where eye contact is key. You are well aware that eye contact in any conversation is important, as it shows you care and it's the respectful thing to do. What you probably didn't know is that by following one's eye direction, you can essentially read their mind.

Visuals move their eyes in three basic directions. When their eyes go up and to the right, they are thinking about future information. Let's use the car salesman analogy. You ask the prospective customer, *"What are you looking for in your new car?"* If their eyes go up and to the right (from your vantage point; in the prospect's eyes, they are looking up and to their left), they are constructing or creating a visual for what they are looking for, possibly a new sedan, convertible, or minivan for their expanding family. If eyes venture up and to the left (their right), they are recalling something that they saw in the past. Lastly, if they give you the blank stare, it's not that they have checked out...quite the opposite, as they are translating what you are saying into a picture for them to understand faster.

Listen to the words they are saying. Sometimes the whole "staring someone dead in the eyes," thing can be difficult for people I have coached, so if this is the case, the words coming out of the prospective client's or business partner's mouth give you an easier angle. I would note that this is one of those things you are going to have to get over if you are truly trying to be the best salesman or saleswoman you know; at the same time, this is a marathon and not a sprint, so learn in baby steps, my friend! Visuals will give you cues like using the word "look" (*this looks great to me!*), "'I see" (*I see what you mean*), or "view" (*here's my view of the situation*). There are many other examples out there, but the point is that visuals will tell you who they are by the words they prefer to use. If they think in visual terms, the prospect will tell you by describing to you exactly what is going through his or her mind.

If you want a couple arrows for your visual quiver, these are strategies you are going to want to use or have at the ready:

1. Draw, draw, draw! Illustrations of ideas on paper are going to be mission critical.
2. Don't be afraid to talk with your hands. You will come across as charismatic to the visual you are talking to, and it will allow your prospect to picture whatever message you are getting across.
3. If you are handing your prospect something to visualize (like a paper with charts, graphs, or a fact sheet), hand it off and shut up. When your prospect is done process-

ing what you handed over, the person will re-engage eye contact.
4. Be acutely conscious of what you wear. Some of the best colors to sport would be blues, grays, or purples. Try to avoid the strong reds, yellows, or browns. Obviously if you have met your prospect for the first time, there is no control over what you are wearing (I strongly advise not to change right then and there), so just be cognizant of this fact when you are getting ready for the day.

Lastly, you want to match the visuals' words. This is hands down the most important strategy to use, so if you completely forgot everything you just read, underline this paragraph until your hands bleed. If you match your verbiage with words that mirror who a visual is, the perception of being equal increases substantially. A couple that come to mind would be:

- Do you "see" what I'm talking about?
- What is your "view" on this?
- What is your "vision" when it comes to an end result?

The more sight-based words you use, the better. Visual verbiage with visuals leads to faster, sincere trust which in turn leads to a faster understanding of what the visual person desires, which means a faster closing rate.

AUDITORIES

These people tend to think more with specific sounds. Auditories will analyze your recommendations mostly on the sound of your voice and tone as opposed to what something will look like. Similar to visuals, eye direction will be key and there are three main movements. If their eyes move directly to the right, they are establishing and creating sounds. Go back to the car sales analogy. Ask the prospect, "Where would you want to take this car for a drive most often?" If the eyes move to the right and an answer, "I'd love to take this hot rod on the freeway on Sundays where there is less traffic so I can really hear that engine roar, but I wonder what my wife will say about that," they are hearing what the future will sound like in multiple ways. On the other hand, if the prospect's eyes went to the left, they are hearing past sounds. If you asked something like "Have you ever heard of our new warranty program?" and the prospect looks down and to their left (from your view, down and right), the prospect is asking him or herself if they have heard about it and having a conversation internally. Let that conversation happen and once a realization occurs, the prospect will reengage eye contact with you. As for word usage, auditories will use words such as "sounds" (*that sounds fantastic!*), "say" (*I am loving what you are saying, where to I sign?!*) or "hear" (*I hear what you are saying*).

If you are going to come to the table with some strategies up your sleeve, here is the big one: match what they are saying (just as with visuals). When you are asking if something makes sense, ask the prospect something along the lines of, "Does that *sound* good to you?" or, "Do you like what you are *hearing*?" or, "Is this *music to your ears*?" Matching sound-based words with auditories will get your register to ring a whole heck of a lot faster than utilizing any bogus sales technique you've been lied to about. This is a bit more advanced, but if you are able to speak in riddle or rhyme, auditories *love* that. I'm not saying to suddenly transform into the next Eminem, but if there are a few things that you can mix and weave into your day-to-day sales quiver, it's going to help. Keeping with the car theme, you could say something like "This all-wheel *drive* will allow your daughter to *thrive* on the road." It's not rocket science that my rap career is non-existant, but you get my drift (car pun not intended, but a quality pun nonetheless).

If you run a business or have control over this next strategy, make sure to have appropriate background music on in your place of work. A study done by Wal-Mart showed that when slow music was played throughout the store, sales were significantly higher than when fast music was playing.[6] If your sales process includes an initial meeting and then a meeting to go over the game plan, during the initial meeting you should ideally have classical music playing in the background and during the presentation meeting, if you know the prospect is auditory, faster-paced songs could hasten their decision to act quickly.

Lastly with regards to auditories, if you are in a line of sales where it's required to provide a pamphlet or visual to the prospect, more often than not auditories are going to want you to explain things, whereas visuals want to look, take it in, and then reengage.

KINESTHETICS

The last type of person in this chapter is the rare kinesthetic. These are the feeling-based people and only about 5% of the population fit this category, so it is super niche; however, that doesn't mean you can simply glance over this group. These are the people that live and die by how they feel. They will choose to work with someone or buy something by their feeling in that moment. This should not be confused with someone who buys without much thought and goes off of immediate feeling. There is still a ton of depth in thought with kinesthetics, but at the end of the day, they live and die by whether they felt hot or cold in just about every experience they have had. Unlike the other two types of people, these people have one eye direction: down and to the left (down and to their right). This will tell you they are in operation: feeling-based mode.

Just as the prior two types of people, words matter with kinesthetics. You may hear things like, "Whoa, that really *touched* me," or ,"This is how I *feel* about the situation." A couple tips worth noting would be to:

1. Use sentences such as, "How does that *grab* you?" or, "What is your *impression* of this?" or, "Would you like me to *touch* base with you in the coming days or next week?" Remember: match words with *feelings*.
2. If possible, give them something to touch or feel. Because their mental focus is on feelings, by giving prospects something to touch around an idea, it brings the emotion of it to a tangible forefront in their minds (since they are, in the most literal sense, touching whatever is the point of sale). If a prospect reaches out to grab a pamphlet as you are talking, that can be a telltale sign you are dealing with a kinesthetic.

Now that you know the three types of people, think about this for a second: Do you see how by simply discovering who someone is, you become an infinitely better guide and educator? Do you think your prospect or business partner would develop a bond with you at a faster rate than just about any other competition out there? A common myth in sales is that people buy the product you are selling first. That is absolutely incorrect. *People buy trust in you first and the product second.*

I wanted to make sure this was a chapter that set the tone for the coming chapters in the section *What to do to make them a client* because this knowledge is something I learned much later in my professional career, and had I known this beforehand, my revenue numbers would have grown at an infinitely faster pace. There are a couple rules with compounding and the first is to start early. Unfortunately, I cannot go back and change the past, but now that *you* have this at your fingertips, the next few chapters will come infinitely easier and your sense of (financial) fulfillment will be here before you know it.

If you have been in sales for some time and are simply not closing more business, this chapter could single-handedly be your saving grace, as I have coached countless people who were simply incorrectly mirroring and matching the prospective client's or business partner's type. It's as simple as that: the better you understand what makes your prospect or business partner want to buy or work with you in some capacity, the closer you are to making some serious money.

Chapter 7:
The Initial Meeting

When it comes to *CAPitalizing Your Sales*, the initial meeting is why most of you bought this book for in the first place. This is where your experience will be gained and the more meetings you have, the more experienced you will be. The old thinking of, "The older you are, the more experience you have," does not stand up to the new age of thought in sales, where, "The more initial meetings you have, the more experience you have and the better salesperson you will be." The art of conducting an initial meeting with a prospective buyer or business partner is going to be key, but you will quickly realize that instead of "closing," you will feel as though you are educating and guiding whoever it is you are talking to, and that feeling of sincere help trumps all hard closers out there (plus, you won't come home every day feeling like you need to shower off the filth of insincere sales techniques...trust me... those are the WORST).

To figure out how to tackle an initial meeting with a prospect, I am going to go through a hypothetical first meeting I have with a possible new client that comes through my business's door. You are probably thinking, "*Isn't this going to turn off those that possibly want to work with you in the future?*" My answer: absolutely not and, if anything, it will move the needle that much closer in a positive direction. I have absolutely zero to hide! Know that when you are absolutely in love with what you do and know deep down in your core that what you provide will help others for the better, there's nothing sleazy, manipulating, or egregious about what you are about to read. It's all about using techniques we discussed in the last chapter (as well as some others I will share with you in this chapter) for the greatest good in providing overall net-positivity to the person across from you.

When someone comes into my office, my amazing teammate seats them and asks if they want anything to drink. Back when I started out, I did everything and if you haven't done every step of the sales process, not only will you not have a complete understanding of **CAPitalizing Your Sales**; there is a zero percent chance those that you hire in your business will ever holistically respect you. I remember that when I interviewed Forbes' lead columnist in their manufacturing division, Jim Vinoski, he told me he once interviewed a founder of one of the most successful lumber companies in the United States. When he asked the founder what was the best piece of advice he could give his readers, he replied, *No matter how far I progressed, I never left the factory floor.* If you started out in business by jumping into the executive level and wonder why the deep-down respect is not felt by your employees, reread that quote.

After the prospective client or clients get situated, it's my time to shine! If the meeting is in person, I like to make sure the client found the office easily and find out how their day is going. It's no different than any interaction, except eventually you will be paid for your services if you do an appropriate job of listening to their needs, and, in the second meeting, repeating those needs accordingly and solving their specific situations. I say this because, far too often, people immediately think they need to sell whoever it is they are talking to, right out of the gate. RELAAAAX. Don't think of this as a sales meeting; think of it as a conversation you would have with anyone you already know, only this time you are discovering everything you need to about this new person. Once the rapport has been built, I kick things off by asking a starting question, which is something like:

- What's on your mind that you'd like to talk about?
- How can I be of service?
- What can I do to help you the most?

This question gets the ball rolling for the meeting, as your prospects have taken the time to come see you and want to see what you can do to help resolve their pressing need. This also brings up a great point: the fact that someone has set aside time to see you (or log onto a video call) tells you the prospect is already interested in what you are offering, so that's all the more reason to keep calm and have a comfortable conversation.

Once that initial question is asked, I tend to shut it (and you should too) because what comes next is the list of things your prospective client wants you to sell them. Seriously...it's that straightforward. Let's keep going with a hypothetical in my office and then I will open it up to how you can pivot into any industry.

Let's say that someone comes in and says they are:

1. Nervous about if they will have enough to retire on.
2. Curious as to what their tax situation will be for the next five years.
3. Wanting to know when to turn on their social security retirement income.

As they are saying these things, I am doing *very* little (if any) talking and I am writing down every major need the prospect is telling me they need to have filled in order to move forward with me. After I write everything down, before I go through questions specific to my industry, I repeat those questions to them:

Before we move forward, I want to make sure I heard you correctly. You told me you want to:

See something that will ease your nervousness in regards to the unknown about if you will have enough money to retire on?

Have your tax question answered on what your tax situation will look like over the next five years?

Know when to turn on your social security retirement income?

Did I hear your major needs correctly? (They say yes.) If your plan shows these three answers accordingly, would those be the questions that you need answered that would have you move in the direction of working with us? (If yes, congratulations, you basically just sold them. If no, ask them what other questions they would like to have answered so that you would feel confident in moving forward with your services).

Notice how, throughout this entire thing, I am not giving a single answer. Now is not the time. For starters, it's poor salesmanship to give away the whole farm before you've been paid. More importantly, you want to pay respect to your prospects' needs by thoroughly thinking about how you will best serve them and that's how you spend the time between the initial meeting and the presentation meeting. The larger the type of sale (financial planning, buying/selling a business, taxes or legal, buying/selling a home just to name a few), the longer the sales cycle, so don't feel like you have to hard close someone right then and there. Besides, the more you ask questions and match their type of person with appropriate verbal cues, the more they will want to buy from you before that meeting is done. I have had a couple moments in my career where the prospect didn't even care what the plan showed: they were already all-in just on the connection and by the time they came in to go over their plan, it was more a formality than a typical presentation meeting.

When it comes to gathering as many questions (needs) as possible, the more, the merrier, but you want to get at least three. According to a study by LIMRA research:

1. There is a 35% client retention rate over five years with one product or service.
2. Two products=56% chance of retention over five years.
3. Three or more products=92% chance of retention over five years.[7]

If you replace "product or service" with need, you just discovered the easiest path to closing more business: by helping those across the table from you in as many ways as humanly possible.

During this initial meeting, if you already know whoever it is that you are speaking to, there are many techniques you simply won't be able to use because...well...they know you, so they can tell whether you are being yourself or not. If that's the case, treat them like any other friend and just ask them what they want and give it to them already! (Kind of kidding, but also kind of dead serious). If this is a prospect that you just met or is a referral (which we will get into later in the book) who you know a little but don't consider a friend, the following techniques can be extremely helpful.

MATCHING AND PACING

When you are listening to your prospect speak, not only are you tuning into the type of person that he or she is, you should also be locking into their tone and speech pattern. This can be difficult when you are as excited as ever to scream to the mountaintops how great your service is, but internally take a deep breath and really make sure to tune into what the prospect is saying, as well as how they are saying it. If they have a high-pitched tone, bump your tone up closer to theirs. I'm not saying go pre-pubescent on them, just get close. If they have a low voice, drop yours down. If they are a faster talker, it's a bit easier to match their pace, as often these people like to hear themselves talk, which in the world of sales is music to your ears. I have had meetings where prospects have become clients and I have said at most thirty words. They just kept on talking and the subconscious connection they had in their brain told them I was locked into their needs. If the prospect is a slow talker, simply reiterate that deep breath I told you about and remind yourself to go at their pace. Admittedly, I have to remind myself of this last one more often than not because I am a go-go type of guy, so know you are not alone if you have to do the same as me!

MIRRORING

The moment a prospect sits down in my office, I am analyzing everything about them, including their posture and body language. Regardless of what industry you are in, mirroring is one of the most valuable and easiest techniques for you to use. Let's say someone came into my office and has a slight slouch in posture. Am I going to sit up tall and stiff like a plank? Nope...I'm going to (subtly) mirror the slouch. If the meeting is progressing and the prospects cross their legs, I will gradually do the same. If one leans back, I will lean back. It's *really* that easy. You may be thinking to yourself that this sounds super manipulative. Yes, it can be used inappropriately, but you are not one of those bad eggs out there. You are one of the good ones, so being the ethical sales master that you are, you are not only using this for the prospect's greater good, you will get to be *so* good at this that the prospect will never notice. It's an elegant dance. It is easy to learn but difficult to master. If you are curious how delayed your mirroring should be, there is no set time, but I give myself and coaching clients a range of ten to twenty seconds. Ideally, if you can go thirty seconds or so, you are going to be leaps and bounds ahead of just about any competition you come across; however, you don't want to shift your focus from the main task at hand (intently listening to the prospect's needs) to counting to thirty to cross your arms.

One quick point on body leaning. Generally speaking when a prospect is leaning back, I'd say eight out of ten times that is *not* great because that will tell you either they are no longer interested (game over) or you may have misunderstood their needs or the type of person they are. The other two times could simply mean they are more comfortable, but generally if that is the case, the lean-back follows up with something like, "All right, where do I sign up?" If a prospect leans *forward*, that tells you that they are interested. You combine that interest with an elegant mirrored forward lean, you got yourself a surefire sale.

One common technique people like to use in initial meetings is starting off by going over agendas about what will be discussed. I used to do this and it felt too corporate-y to me (and yes, corporate-y is a *highly* sophisticated sales term…joking of course). Instead, what I like to do is tell the prospect something like this:

> It's safe to say that we all know why you are here today and before we dive into the good stuff, I want to first lay out our team's general process on how we work with people. That way, if you decide to hire us, there are no surprises. Today, I am here to

gather as much information about you as possible. No answers, just questions and gather information. Between now and our next meeting, I will go back to the lab (what I refer to as my office) and write up your plan with all of your questions answered. At that time, we will go over costs, next steps and that is the time where people say they are either aboard the CAPitalize Circle of Trust or we're not for them. We don't delay and kick the can down the road and we'd love to serve you, but we understand we are not for everyone. We only ask that, at the end of that meeting, we have our decision and then we can all move forward. Do you have any questions about our process I just laid out before we dive into the fun stuff of today's meeting?

Notice a couple things in this informal agenda. I get every surprise out of the way and lay it all out there so there are no unknowns. I sprinkle in humor (it never hurts to get someone to smile). Most importantly, if there are objections to the process, the prospect is not wasting their time and you are not wasting yours. This last part can sound a bit aggressive, but it is simple: your existing client's time is just as important as your prospective client's time. Even if you don't have clients and everyone is a prospective client, trust me when I say that you don't want someone complaining and nitpicking absolutely everything you do for them. It's hard enough to give everything you got for your clients that think the world of you; imagine how much more difficult it will be if you are doing this for a client that thinks you're a transaction.

There are SO many ways to conduct an initial meeting and for business clients where I go out to speak to their sales staff,

I go over various other techniques like specific industry basic probing questions, the "Let's Assume" technique, Broad Brush Trial Closing, and Up Front Closing. But what I laid out to you is what I use every single day and, as you have already read, my business's revenue speaks for itself.

Now that you know the ins and outs of the initial meeting (and have your eager prospect on the calendar to come back to see what you have in stored), it's time to enter the presentation meeting and start closing some sales!!!

Chapter 8:
How to conduct a presentation meeting

The time has come. Your prospective new client is back to hear what you have to say and make the decision: yes or no. This is where the register will either be literally rung OR you two part ways and you walk away with nothing to show for it. It is time to laser in, lock and load, and learn to close.

In many ways, if you conducted your initial meeting appropriately, this meeting should be the cherry on top, as the prospects should essentially be coming in to reaffirm the decision they made to work with you after the initial meeting's conclusion. How am I so sure about this?

Here's why: When the initial meeting was in full swing, you were consistently asking questions that they were telling you *how* they wanted them answered. In the world of finance, if someone told me they needed to see some growth in their portfolio, guess what? The plan will show them growing accordingly (and prudently, of course). If you are an architect and the client asked you to put pen to paper on how their new dream kitchen will look, you best believe that you are going to give them exactly what they asked for because otherwise it's a no-brainer that the prospect is not going to hire you.

The key difference between the obvious and not-so-obvious is *how* you are delivering this information. Remember: at the first meeting you learned the type of person you are talking to and took mental notes on how they best communicate. You also gathered every major question they wanted to have answered in order of importance, so at the very beginning of the meeting, you know exactly how to quarterback their order of importance to a T.

When I have a meeting where I am going over a presentation with a prospective client, I like to start it with something like this:

> *Alrighty Mr. & Mrs. Client, before we dive into the festivities of today's meeting and answer all of your heart's desires, I want to refresh our minds about where we left off last meeting so that we can answer your most important questions. Going back to where we left off, your most important questions you wanted to have answered in order to decide to hire yours truly are:*
>
> *1. Knowing if you could live off of $6,000 per month in retirement.*
> *2. What your financial plan looks like in terms of where to invest your money accordingly.*
> *3. Understanding of the proper game plan to make sure your kids inherit as much money as possible.*

Before we dive into the belly of the beast (commonly referred to as your CAPitalized Financial Plan), were these the main questions you needed answered in order to decide to work with me?

If the client says these are the main and only questions, fantastic, and I would proceed with the plan accordingly. If the client has more questions, simply add them to the list and as you go through your presentation, continuously go back to ensure each question is answered, especially the ones you just added. In investing, there is a term referred to as recency bias, where one tends to overemphasize the importance of a certain experience or latest information in terms of predicting future events. This is no different in sales: if the clients bring up something like this to you in the moment, that is the most pressing thing on their minds. If you can tailor your presentation in real time to get them to understand that you know *exactly* what they need (especially if it has *just* been discovered), you will compound your closing rate to an immense degree. Not only do you know what the prospective client needs, you know how they communicate, can regurgitate their needs in the best way they know how to receive information AND can do so with information they *just* provided you all of ten seconds ago. That, my friends, is the epitome of a CAPitalizer and a CAPitalize Your Sales master!

For larger sales items, such as financial planning, buying a home, looking to sell a business or getting your estate in order, know that you may have to have several presentation meetings. Most sales gurus out there will tell you that once you go through with the methods described above, they will magically convert your prospects into clients on the spot. I am not saying that for the most part these prospects are ready to rock and roll after the presentation meeting is complete, but the larger the sale (as well as greater the importance in the prospects' minds), the longer it will take. It's just the nature of the beast. If that's the case, how do you continue the conversation until you ring the register?

Let's say you are an attorney looking to provide a complex estate plan to your (soon to be) largest client. If they are ready to rock, you know what to do and if for whatever reason you don't, we will conclude this chapter by going over how to keep that ball rolling. If the prospect is not ready to commit and wants to have time to look over it, most attorneys I have seen COMPLETELY drop the ball here, as they will say something like, "That sounds great. Take home your documents and give them a read and, when you are ready, call my office back and we will schedule a time to go over any questions you may have."

This is the sales equivalent of nails on a chalkboard.

For starters, I hate to tell you this...but the moment someone walks out of your office and you give that guidance, you might as well kiss them goodbye because they simply will not care as much as you will about getting this complete. In their defense, why should they? They don't know how much value you are providing them in relation to what you know, so by definition they would be in the dark compared to your plethora of knowledge in your specific field. Saying it another way, they will forget just about everything you said and you will never get that call again.

If I were coaching an attorney in this scenario (which I have done *many* times), I would close out the meeting like this:

> *I completely understand that you need more time to look this over and, as a standard procedure, I actually recommend clients do exactly what I am telling you to do, which is to go home, read this over, and we will set up a time before you are out the door to come back into the office to go over any questions and decide on you proceeding with your estate plan or not. With our clients, we don't like to take the follow-up meeting out too far, as we don't want you forgetting to do your homework on top of you losing track of the importance of what you want to have answered promptly. Because of this, let's look at your calendar and see what your schedule looks like next week at the same time. We would prefer to have you come back into the office, but if that is more inconvenient, we would be happy to have this be a follow up call. Which one would you prefer?*

In this situation, you gave your prospective client the choice of how to meet with you to follow up, as well as planting a sense of urgency in their mind so that they reiterate subconsciously to themselves how important this decision is. By giving them the flexibility of how to meet with you, you also provided them with the fact that you are flexible regardless of how they wish to proceed with the follow-up. You are also letting them know (without being direct) that you value both your time and the prospect's time and are not one to waste anyone's time, especially your current clients who already trust you. Occasionally, the prospect may push back regarding wanting to control when to call you back and the one thing I am *not* about is kicking the can down the road. There are a ton of techniques out there to press and press and press until the prospect caves and puts something on the calendar (assuming they are pushing back and insisting that they will call you). Despite the strategies I have listened to and learned in the past, I am just going to cut to the chase: if it gets to that point, you are wasting your time. I would say two times out of ten, those people in fact do call you back (and if they do, it is most likely to say that they are ready to become clients of yours), but the other eight...you don't want them as clients anyway. One thing to remember is that if it is extremely difficult to convert someone into a client at the get-go, it's going to be just as difficult to keep them continually satisfied with your incredible services, so it's best to cut ties when you see these red flags.

If we assume the prospect is ready to rock and roll, depending on your line of work, you either put the pen to paper on the spot or set up a time a day or so down the road to have them either hop into your office to sign paperwork, or jump on a call and properly complete their documents electronically from the comfort of their own home. Ideally, once you know the prospect is all in, the sooner they sign, the better. Before we move on to the next chapter, there are a few final aspects of the presentation meeting that are worth noting.

Oftentimes if you are in a line of sales where the sale is on a smaller/quicker scale (fashion or restaurant) or mid-size (auto), more often than not your initial meeting and presentation meeting are back-to-back. If that is the case, instead of getting the prospect, "back on the books" to go over their next moves, things will flow naturally in that interaction. Let's take the auto industry as an example. For those in the mid-size type of sales industry, one tip I have coached clients on is to go over the "initial meeting" (first half of your meeting) with gathering information you need to close the prospect and then have the prospect go sit down and make themselves comfortable so you can go back and do the best diligence possible. By the time you come back (generally after ten to fifteen minutes or so), in the mind of the prospect, that is enough of a subconscious difference in timing so that they are geared towards the "presentation" portion of your get-together. With cars, the prospects will appreciate that you took the time to go dig into some research instead of hurrying them into the first car you see on the floor to sell them. Obviously you have to read the room if the prospect comes in and says, "I'm looking for a Ford F-150," and the F-150 is sitting right in front of your face, but when in doubt, take the extra few minutes to separate getting to know the prospect's needs from solving that need with a presentation. You quickly evolve in the prospect's mind from a sleazy salesman to the genuine expert who has sincere patience.

The presentation meeting is where most people think they mess up the most because if the sale isn't closed, they aren't getting paid. This is the farthest thing from the truth. To give you an idea, if you are closing four or five out of every ten sales, you are an absolute Godsend in the world of sales. Too many people focus on the all-in aspect of the presentation meetings while completely forgetting (or ignoring) everything before this chapter. The more initial meetings you book, the better off you will be. Remember: experience is not forged in years you've lived; it's in the number of meetings you have. The more jam-packed your schedule is with possible new sales, the more comfortable you will feel (both in general and in the specific meetings) and the more comfortable you feel, the higher your closing rate will be.

When you know a prospect is ready to be a client, always make sure you lay out the next steps. A common mistake I see people make in this moment is that they ring their register and immediately jump to the next opportunity. This is a CRITICAL error. Think about it: this person likes and trusts you enough to buy from you, so don't you think you have a built-in referral system since you met their expectations (and often then some)? I am a huge believer in, regardless of whether you are in a transactional industry (cars) or service-based industry (CPA or insurance agent) to always....always build a recurring consistent touch point with your new client or customer. In the next chapter, we will be discussing how you keep these new clients or customers coming back for more.

Chapter 9:
Now that they're a client, keep them coming back!

Think for just a moment about how far you have come. If you have followed the CAPitalize Your Sales Framework up until this point, this means that you have made a sale! I remember like it was yesterday the first time I ever landed a client, and it was the most euphoric feeling in the world. For those who have never been in the world of sales, it is impossible to explain the feeling, as a HUGE blast of excitement rushes over you to the point where you are about to scream! I pray that you have this feeling over and over and over again for many years to come; however, this is where most sales rookies miss a gigantic (and easy) opportunity.

This is what happens to 99% of rookies:

1. The client or customer is closed.
2. The paperwork is signed.

3. Handshakes are made.
4. The new client or customer is out the door.

Do you see what was missed?

Unfortunately, most of you that have been here in the past missed the beauty of *recurring* sales. If you want to know what separates the one percent in sales from the rest of the pack, this is it, so ingrain this into your brain at all costs.

Recurring sales can be much more obvious in service-based businesses where the professional has to consistently reevaluate clients' scenarios, but even if you are in a transactional line of work, you can choose to make it a recurring opportunity. Regardless of whether you are a car salesman, social media consultant, merger and acquisition broker, builder, etc., once you know your product better than anyone, you'll know when it is time to check in with your new-found clients and customers. Better yet, even if you don't necessarily *need* to check in with your new cheerleaders that rang your register with smiles on their faces, they don't know the difference. So by separating yourself from the pack and following up more so than anyone they have ever worked with, you will 100% re-ring your register almost automatically.

When you are closing the client or customer, set the stage for your new relationship. People buy from you because of your relationship more so than what they are actually buying, and what checking in with them does is sincerely compound the quality of that relationship. Let's assume you are in a service-based business, like a health insurance specialist for companies. Once the sale is closed, say something like this:

> Mr./Mrs. Client, I am super excited that I am honored enough to be a steward of your and your business's trust and I cannot wait for a lifetime of consistently earning that trust. What I like to do is lay out the coming year so that there are not surprises. Once a year, we will meet to go over your business's health insurance plan in a much more comprehensive way; however, one thing that I do differently with my clients is meet on a quarterly basis to check in on your benefits from a 50,000 foot level. Not only does this help in staying on top of any issues that may arise; I also get to truly understand the ins and outs of your business, which will further assist me in being the best health insurance specialist I can be for you and your firm. With that, let's look at our calendars and get our first thirty-minute check in on the books. What does your day look like on [day, month] and what time works best for you?

The fact that your client or customer is already all-in on you almost guarantees that they will want to keep the good vibes rolling with your award-winning service. A common question I get at this point is, "*Is that all?*" and, for the most part, the answer is...well...yeah! People think it is always "The next trick in the book" regarding sales, but during these conversations, you will first and foremost *always* make sure whatever it is that you do for them professionally is taken care of to the best of your abilities. After that, the greatest part of sales comes alive: you get to know your customers and clients for who they are, not how much they can pay you. Remember: the more genuine the connection, the louder your register will ring!

For industries where sales are truly transactional, such as car sales, this can feel uncomfortable at first because more often than not, the industry is geared to sell, sell, sell and not sell-and-build-relationships. Another issue is the fact that, let's face it, once you buy a car, chances are you are not going to buy another one for a while. Even if your customer leases a car, it's going to be a couple of years until the customer comes back for another vehicle. My advice would be to ignore that discomforting feel and get them on *your* schedule. Regardless of whether it is every ninety days (you will read why this is ideal in chapter 12), every six months, or once a year, the fact that you go out of your way to not be normal and emphasize a high level of customer service will make you more money than you could ever dream of.

The point of this recurrence is the human aspect of things. Later in the book, I will provide you with strategic ways to ask for more business (this is all coming to you in the next section), but you are probably asking why I don't give this to you now? There are several reasons.

The first reason: don't make the same mistake I made. I missed out on that genuine connection piece. I was an absolute machine and, in the midst of the machinery, I couldn't marinade in genuine interaction. Had I known that it was oftentimes best just to take a deep breath and not have to always be in sales mode, the compounding of my goodwill would have occurred much sooner.

The second reason dovetails from reason numero uno in the fact that if you are a voracious sales machine, often it becomes disingenuous (or can appear so to your client or customer). There was a moment in my career where I was hitting on all cylinders and the client said something along the lines of, "Let's first get my situation all squared away and then we can talk about introductions after the fact." I can't tell you how horrible I felt and that evening, even though I was supposed to be elated about closing my new client (which was a big one for me at the time), that *one* moment made me feel incredibly dirty... the "I needed to take a shower for hours" type of dirty. Even though my intentions were pure, perception was reality and, in that instance, it was *not* great.

Now that you know what I did to mess up my great moments, don't do the same. Instead, enjoy these sales and genuinely connect with your new clients and customers. Let the conversations flow freely after business is taken care of (but remember to always get the next meeting on the calendar). You will be forever thankful you did.

Take a moment to step back and take in everything you have learned up until this point. You now know everything in the CAPitalize Your Sales funnel from networking all the way down to ringing your register! In a way, you have become the ultimate hunter of sales and, best of all, you don't feel slimy about it! The next section is going to move you from making a sale here and there to having a referral pipeline that is going to grow so fast that you will be basking in the rays of financial euphoria!

Let's get into the art of how to build a top-tier referral pipeline!

SECTION 3:

How to build a top-tier referral pipeline

Most sales books I have read stop at the chapter you recently completed, as the common misconception with sales is that once the sale is complete, the battle is won. Although the battle is won, the war is *far* from over if you are going to become the greatest sales person you can be. What separates the rookies from the veterans in the world of sales is the art of selling while you sleep. Obviously, I don't mean this in the literal sense (although there was a guy who recorded himself sleeping, posted it on YouTube and has reportedly made *millions* from advertisements...makes you ask yourself what you're doing with your life, right??). What I mean by this is that you can wake up and, in a rolling thirty-day period, the odds of you having a new sales opportunity sent your way will be nearly 100%.

I remember that early in my career, a business partner of mine said something that rings more and more true as the days pass:

The sale starts* after *you close the client.

This is true from both a service perspective and a referral perspective and what's beautiful is that, if you have followed the CAPitalize Your Sales Framework to a T to this point, the relationships you have built have become so enriched and fulfilling that this upcoming section will flow like fine wine.

In this section, you are going to learn:

1. How to further assist your clients or customers with getting to know who else is on their team (and partnering with them).
2. How to master the art of a "Warm" call for a business partner, as this will be *infinitely* easier with common clients or customers.
3. What to do to maximize your referral source right in front of you.
4. The dance of the 90-day cheat code to unlock more sales opportunities without sounding like a sleazeball.

In the world of investing, if you want to know the one commonality in those who have outperformed everyone else, it's that their portfolio is *not* diversified. It is concentrated in a few incredible opportunities and when the bets pay off, those people do incredibly well. Take that mental model and convert it to your clients or customers. Far too often, men and women in sales don't allow themselves to transition from hunter to nurturer. Putting it another way, you will go from searching far and wide for sales opportunities to focusing on the client or customer base that has already bought from you. Part of this is knowing who else is assisting in the line of work that you are in, which you will learn in Chapter 10. You learned a bit about "warm" calling after a networking event earlier on in this book, so Chapter 11 will, in some ways, be a refresher. On the other hand, it is a totally different beast when it comes to working with potential business partners, as it will take months if not *years* to build an incredible relationship. This shouldn't come as a shock to you: think about it for a second. Who in your life have you referred the most business to and why? Sure, they have probably done a wonderful job at whatever they do; however, the deeper reason is the relationship you have built with them. If you are already in business and refer out to a certain person, ask yourself how long it took for you to build that trust. I can guarantee you the best ones took time. There have been instances where I have immediately connected and started referring my clients out in a matter of days, but far too often it is a marathon. In my line of work, my greatest referral source is CPAs and some of my business partners that I have become dear friends with did not start sending me business until *four years into our friendship*. In a perfect world, if business partners that are referral sources become a client or customer of yours, you just hit the jackpot, but in chapter 11, you are going to learn the framework of going from total stranger to building these referral sources beyond your wildest dreams.

    The late Charlie Munger had a quote that did not hit me until later in my career and it 100% topical to your eventual learnings in Chapter 12:

> *It's the work on your desk. Do well with what you already have and the more will come in.*
>
> ~Charlie Munger, Poor Charlie's Almanack?
> The Wit and Wisdom of Charles T. Munger

This chapter will be much more of a reminder of what you are put on this earth to do than a tips and tricks framework, but boy oh boy, is it a chapter that I selfishly wrote for myself as a CONSTANT reminder to focus on what is in front of me. You may not believe me when I tell you this, but there will come a point where you will be able to look at your sales funnel (or business if you run one) and say with relative certainty what you are going to earn on a monthly, quarterly and annual basis. If you are reading this and you are in a service-based business with built-in recurring sales opportunities, this will be extremely easy for you, as you will be able to naturally take your foot off the "hunting" pedal and start the transition to nurturing your clients or customers much more easily. If you are in a transactional type of work like car sales, payroll providers, or fashion, you will have to work a bit harder at this transition, but once you get the hang of it, in many ways, it will come that much more naturally to you. Often the harder you have to work at something, the greater the reward and the more difficult it is to lose whatever it may be. Regardless of your line of work, chapter 12, although not a, "this new strategy/tip/trick" type of chapter, will be a pivotal moment in your sales career (as well as your career in general), so don't skim over it...trust me.

The last chapter of this section, Chapter 13, will take you into a deep dive of the beauty of what I call the ninety-day cheat code. In the previous section, I slipped in a hint of this strategy, but didn't want you to get hooked onto it just yet, as the moral of the book up until this section is to sincerely focus on the genuine quality of your new-found professional and personal relationships. Now that you have done that, at the end of every ninety-day period, there are things you can do to further hasten the referral funnel. This is also where you will start to further your transition in your sales mastery, as you will go from the sales front lines to the five-star sales general you've always wanted to become. The best part of Chapter 13? It's one of the simplest if not *the* simplest strategies you will learn in the CAPitalize Your Sales' Framework (and you will feel *infinitely* better about yourself as you use it).

Now that we have laid out what the next section is going to give you, it's time to get into it. First up: now that you have clients, let's learn who helps in making them succeed alongside you and get to partnering with them!

Chapter 10:

Now that you have clients, learn who helps in making them succeed...and partner with them!

If you are sincerely aiming to be the best salesperson you can be, you are going to have to take some time *not* landing sales left and right. This sounds counterproductive but give me a moment to make my case. There are two types of salespeople out there when it comes to the topic of this chapter:

1. Those who make the sale and move on.
2. Those who make the sale and double down on getting to know every aspect of their new client or customer to figure out how to further help them that much more.

I am going to explain what I mean by going through a couple hypothetical scenarios to give you an idea of what I am talking about. The first one is...well...my own!

In my business of financially planning for families of high net worth and business's retirement plans, it should not come as a shocker that it is *impossible* to succeed in this business alone. Since this is not a solo show, I quickly realized that, once I earned the trust of these families and businesses, I needed to surround myself with the rest of their team. A few examples would be helpful:

For the high net worth families:

1. Someone is doing their taxes (generally a CPA) and so I needed to know who that CPA is.
2. If they have a massive estate plan (fancy way of saying a ton of money and equally as many problems and complexities), an estate attorney created that for them.
3. If they need proper investments in various vehicles like stocks, real estate, or elsewhere, I'd better partner with the right players that could provide my clients with what they desired.

For the businesses whose retirement plans I oversee:

1. A third-party administrator has to write the documents to make the plan real, so there's another arrow I must add to my quiver.
2. The client's business attorney for various business needs.
3. Does that client want health insurance for their company? A company health insurance expert is a must.

Why am I telling you all of this?

When you were starting your sales pursuit, let's take a trip down memory lane to remind you that you had no clients or customers, business partners, money or...frankly...hope. The initial clients or customers, business partners, and sales were just to (in most cases) barely scrape by. As you become more and more seasoned, you start to develop those clients or customers that are the jackpot because they provide you with the majority of your revenue. Even more important, you genuinely enjoy serving them. Through knowing who else assists in their success with your field, if that professional works with them, you find the professional is generally cut from the same cloth. The whole idea of, "You are who you hang out with" rings especially true in business.

If you did not discover who your client's "team" is during your initial meeting, don't worry! If you are meeting with your clients or customers every ninety days (or whatever is most optimal for your business or sales cycle), you can gather that information next time. Let's assume you didn't get this information right off the bat and it's the first recurring get-together. I would kick it off like this if I were coaching someone in my industry:

> *Today, I want you to get in the rhythm of what these get-togethers feel like, as there are meetings of ours where it is going to be just as comprehensive as when we initially brought you on as clients, and others where it is as simple as checking in for five or ten minutes. During our discussion today; however, I would love to start out by getting information on your*

> other financial professionals that help quarterback your personal financial picture. What is the name of your CPA? Tell me about him/her. What is the name of your estate attorney? Tell me about him/her.

After the client tells you about the business partners, I would ask for an introduction like this:

> *These sound like terrific people and it appears that you have a solid relationship with them. One of the aspects of our business that we focus on is surrounding ourselves with the rest of your team so that we can further enhance your overall situation by developing sincere relationships with those that help you thrive. Would it be all right if I gave them a call sometime today after our meeting to introduce myself? I would like to meet them and get to know them better [as well as have them get to know me] so that if we fast-forward a year from now, your overall financial plan is rolling on all cylinders, both directly related and indirectly related to what we provide your family. If you would like, could you let them know I will be contacting them or perhaps an introduction would be more up your alley?*

In the next chapter, we will discuss how these calls and meetings thereafter will play out, but for now, the sole focus is to practice the art of building your referral pipeline from your clients' business partners that work in tandem with you. We call these your *Centers of Influence*.

Let's take another industry as an example...take dentistry. Who would help your business grow indirectly?

- Oral surgeons
- Orthodontists
- Pediatric dentists for kiddos who are graduating to the adult dentists

How would those conversations go? Basically, exactly how a conversation would go with my situation, with the difference in the fact that you will have a *significantly* easier time gaining your fellow professional's trust since your businesses overlap to an immense extent. Getting introductions to those people would be a breeze since dentists have their clients in their chairs for up to an hour...that is plenty of time to chat about everyday life and ask at the end who they would know in any of the respective fields I mentioned in the bullet points above.

There are a number of businesses and industries where it is pretty straightforward as to who will help you in furthering your client's success, but what if you don't know who these people are in your respective line of work? The power of asking and listening will solve that problem almost instantly. The more you ask how you can help your clients or customers, the more they will tell you what they need, regardless of whether it is in your circle of competence or not. If you get to know someone who is not remotely related to your client's or customer's situation where you assist and your client/customer mentions that it would be worth your time meeting them, guess what: you do it. Remember: the fact that this new-found person is most likely similar to your top/favorite client or customer is more than enough to meet up. If people like you, they work with you. It's that simple.

Before we move onto the "warm" calling of chapter 11, it's worth noting something that I wish I knew earlier in my career, as it would have catapulted my overall success at a much faster rate. What I get paid to do by my clients is plan for their future and present with their money, but what set my business skyrocketing is the art of pointing them in the right direction. Said another way, I realized I am not a *planner* but a *pointer*. Most sales professionals ask, *"What can I do to help?"* which is a fine question but most of the time, your clients will not know what that means as it's a super-broad question and catches them off guard. Instead, always continue to ask much more nuanced and niche questions regarding the conversation you are having. If the conversation is leading to your customers being excited about their daughter's birthday party, ask them who they are using for a party planner/baker for the cake/venue/etc. If you are discussing new home additions, ask who is building it out/if they have an architect/painter/contractor/HVAC specialist/etc. It's counterintuitive for sales professionals to ask about anything outside of the box that rings the register, but by practicing this little bonus of a final paragraph to this chapter, you quickly build up a powerful rolodex of business partners that will always think of you first AND...because you'll be learning about so many newfound needs...you will never stop learning, which is worth more than any sale you will ever land.

Chapter 11:

"Warm" calling to set up meetings with your soon-to-be new business partners

I f you remember back to Chapter 3 where you learned how to CAPitalize on "Cold" Calling off of networking events, Chapter 11 will have a similar feel, only it will feel easier for several reasons. First, you have an immediate interest in common: your client or customer. Second, unlike Chapter 3 where you are still in the figuring-out-how-to-partner-with-a-total-stranger mode, here you don't have to second-guess how business can be cross-pollinated. Third, you have an instant probing question in the fact that, somehow, this professional came in contact with your client or customer.

Curious how to start a conversation like this? It's actually pretty simple. Try something like this:

> Hi, is this [name of person]? My name is Chris Panagiotu, [client in common's] Financial Planner and they mentioned that you do their [name of service] and have amazing things to say about you. The reason why I am calling is I would love to set up a time to get to know more about your business and how you serve clients, as I have a number of clients that are just like [client in common] and if you are anything like them, I know you are fantastic! I want to send my clients/customers to like-minded people, but before I do that, I like to truly get to know them. When would be a good time for you, as I would love to come down to your office and get to know more about you?

Sometimes at the end of these types of calls, I would recommend you also say it would be great to show the professional what you do for the common client so that you and the professional can work together in the best possible way for the common good of the client or customer. If you decide to say this (you have to read the conversation to see if it flows accordingly), make sure you "soft close" the professional, which is a fancy way to ask if that would be all right. If they say yes in a brief manner (i.e., Yea, ok, sure...) chances are that there won't be a tremendous amount of interest from that person when you initially meet. That is not a bad thing at all...in fact, I could argue that it will make you that much better in the sales game because if you convert them from nearly out the door to a referral partner for life, you have taken in everything this book has had to offer and perfected it! On the other hand, if they are interested and sincerely sound like it could be valuable for them to see what you do for their client, that is a surefire way to land one of the most valuable referral partners of your career. The bonus is if they say something along the lines of: "...this would be super helpful for *me* to learn for my own personal situation as well." You get a couple referral partners as clients or customers and read the next chapter, 12...it will be game over in the best possible way!

Let's assume you have this professional on your calendar. Similar to early on in your study of **CAPitalizing Your Sales**, you know that your goal is to learn *everything* about that professional. A few examples (out of an infinite amount):

- Family
- Hobbies
- Literal profession
  - What they actually do
  - Process
  - Who to talk to for what
  - Niche if they have one
  - Ideal client
  - Seasonality to their business
- What they look for in a professional like yourself (and then provide them exactly what they want)
- Where they went to college
- Schedule
- Goals
  - Professional
  - Personal
- What they like to eat
- Are they morning, afternoon or evening people?

I could go on and on, but the more you get to know about them, the greater the chance you will find ways to connect. This list is a solid list to start with and...whatever you do...do *not* take notes on these things while you are talking. I cannot tell you how disingenuous it is when I meet with possible business partners and I look across the table and the notepad reads, "*Chris likes this, Chris likes that, make sure to bring this up here/there, etc.*" The more you genuinely listen, the less you will need to write down because your memory will truly become a steel trap. If you are nervous about missing something important, simply excuse yourself for a second, whip out your phone, input a couple key words in your notes for later, and immediately jump back to honing in on every word out of this professional's mouth.

Ideally, you want to learn everything about them and indirectly *force* themselves to ask what it is you do for your common client or customer in interest and for your clients or customers in general. If time allows and the conversation is flowing accordingly, that is a great time to show them what you do. In a perfect world, however, save that grand reveal for the next time you two meet. If you could control it, say something like this (as it will most likely be towards the end of the initial meeting):

> *You know (name of professional/business partner), I would absolutely love to show you what I specifically do for (client or customer in common); however, I am looking at the time and unfortunately, I have to get to my next meeting. With that being said, I not only want to continue this conversation; I'd like to pro-*

> pose something I think you would enjoy. I have thoroughly enjoyed getting to know more about you and your business and want to treat you like my top business partners, where I meet with them every ninety days. Since you are a (morning/afternoon/evening) type of person and you mentioned that (day of the week and time during the day) works best for you, I want to set up something recurring once a quarter starting three months from now on (a day and time that works best for them). Let's have you come to my office since I know you would like to learn more about what it is I do for (client in common) and from that meeting on, we can call/text each other the day or two before and see if we want to meet at either of our offices or mix it up with a (name something you know they would enjoy i.e. a walk/golf/drinks at their favorite bar/etc.). How does that sound?

By that point, they are going to be so all in, they would think you are their new best friend (which, in some cases, is true!) You get them on the calendar and you got yourself a referral partner.

Before we move on to the next chapter that will *really* rev your referral engine, I first want to give you a couple bonus endings to how these meetings could conclude. First, if this professional is hot to trot and you sense they *really* want to know what you do for your client in common, I would ask them if they would want to come by your office/place of work sooner than next quarter. If that's the case, ask in a way similar to this:

> So I know we got a recurring meeting on the books and I am super excited to continue this new-found friendship, but I can

> *also sense that you really wanted to see what I do for (client in common). Since that's the case, would you want to look at your calendar and see if sometime next week you'd want to come down to the office/place of work; that way I can show you and you won't be bursting with curiosity for an additional ninety days?*

This is a 50/50 in terms of the new-found business partner wanting to meet sooner, but I can guarantee you that if they are extremely eager to get something back on the books, you landed an absolute gold mine. Another bonus finisher would be asking your new best buddy if you could call your client/customer in common to let them know that the meeting was fantastic and that you and your business partner cannot wait to work together on your client's/customer's behalf. Most of the time, it's a no-brainer and the business partner will say that's no problem. Every once in a while, they might laugh and poke fun, as it may seem silly to them to give you permission to chat with your already-client/customer in common. A subtle (yet highly effective) response to that would be:

> *I know it may sound silly since we already work with (client/customer in common), but just as I always ask for permission from my clients/customers, I do the same for business partners, as I value you and your word just as much as (client/customer in common).*

Jokingly agree, but then remind them their word is just as valuable. Your business partner will never forget that.

Up until this point, of this section, you have learned just about everything you need to know *ancillary* about building a top-tier referral pipeline. This next chapter will educate you on mastering the art of what to say to plant the referral seeds into your clients,' customers,' and business partners' minds.

Chapter 12:
Your top referral source is in front of you: now what?

You should feel fantastic knowing that sales is not what you thought it was. Gone are the days where you have to hard-sell someone and back them into a corner or play with your possible customers' or clients' emotions and sell of their emotional lack-of-knowledge as to what you are doing. There is a strong chance that your closing rate has skyrocketed if you have implemented what I have laid out for you in CAPitalize Your Sales's Framework. The best part of all of this is that you have come to realize that sales should not feel like what you have traditionally believed. It's true that the more sincere you are and passionate about what you do, the money will come (and since you have absorbed everything this book has to offer up until this point, your bank account either should already show this or you can see the financial tsunami barreling towards you.) With all of that said, there is a way (in fact, several ways) for you to ask for referrals and it is paramount that you master this step, as it will be the ultimate seed-planter that will take what you have already produced in your sales career and snowball it by at least 3 times...I'm dead serious.

First, it's worth noting what *not to do*. As the late-and-great Charlie Munger once said: *"all I want to know is where I'm going to die so I'll never go there."*[8] In sales (as well as life in general), I have learned that far too often people look for the things to do in order to be successful, but that road is infinitely more difficult to travel. Make it easy on yourself. If you know what *not* to do and avoid those no-gos at all times, by definition you can't help but become successful. It really is that easy.

Now that you have that diamond of tangential advice out of the way, let's get back to knowing what not to say. When I coach sales professionals or business owners on this, the most common mistake when asked how to ask for referrals is something along the lines of this:

> *If you know of anyone that needs my services, please keep me top of mind.*

This grinds my teeth it's so cringy. There is SO much wrong with this. Most of the time, this is asked at the very end of a meeting and 99% of people remember what was first discussed and the last thing said on their way out the door, so if you said something like this and the customer and client only remembers *that*, they are either going to completely forget it because it gives them zero guidance or they will leave with the taste in their mouth that you are becoming a sleazy salesman. Remember that the name of the CAPitalize Your Sales' game is genuine sincerity.

On top of the reasons you just read, what also follows is the fact that most of the time, not only was that the last thing your client/customer heard, if there is no follow-up next meeting (which we will discuss at length in the next chapter), that is the only thing that they will remember and that is the kiss of death. Subconsciously, they will go out of their way *not* to refer you opportunity. Think about it: why would anyone refer someone that they felt uncomfortable around (even if it was only the last 20 seconds of the previous interaction?)

Before you read on, I want you to take a moment and ask yourself how you think you should ask for referrals? I was kind enough to eliminate the hard not-to-do, so you are one step closer to the promised lands of the art of the ask. Do you think this would work?

These are the type of people I work with (describe your ideal client). If you know of anyone that fits this description, please send them my way.

You are getting warmer, but unfortunately this is a no. Don't get me wrong, it is much better than the first try, as further educating your clients on who you serve is by no means a turn off, as it's important to re-enlighten your clients from time to time. The end; however, was basically a carbon copy of bad from the first attempt.

What about this?

> *These are the types of people I work with (describe your ideal client). Now that you know this, who do you know that fits this description?*

We're getting closer and closer, as the second part is certainly better than the previous two attempts, but does it give you that warm-and-fuzzy feeling that would want you to refer yourself? Yep...me neither.

One final attempt:

> *We are growing and getting more selective with who we are wanting to serve and this is our ideal client/customer (describe your ideal client or customer). We want to work with those that are just like our top clients/customers, which you are! I wanted to ask who you would know that is in a similar situation to you that we could serve?*

This is a much better crack at it, but because I know you are getting impatient and want to jump to the magical phrase (or variations of the phrase), I will save you the frustration and further mind-teasing, as this is still not good enough.

Are you ready? Prepare yourself... Here is the magic:

> *Before we get you all squared away for your next meeting, I wanted to first tell you something and ask about a thought of yours between now and next time we get together. My team and*

I have sincerely appreciated serving you and we are excited that, due to our success in our company, we are beginning to become more selective with who we serve. We have been letting our top-tier clients know this (which, of course, you are one of them!) and wanted to ask something of you. This doesn't have to be now or even next meeting, but I wanted to leave you with a question: who do you know that would appreciate a relationship similar to what you have with us?

Boom.

Let's break this down, as there is a lot to unpack.

Right off the bat, you made it *not* the focal point of the end of the conversation, which is what most sales people do. The client or customer will have in their minds that this is a quick mention and ask, which anyone has 20-30 seconds for. You first remind them how much you and your team value them as people, not just as another client. Everyone wants to be a part of success and you have let them know that they are both an integral part of your success while also reminding them in the same breath that they are one of your top clients and, because of that, you trust them enough to make an ask that you are not asking everyone else. Lastly (and most importantly), you are not asking for a direct referral; *you are asking for a relationship similar to the winner of a relationship you and your client/ customer already have.* You did <u>not</u> back them into any corner. You did not force them to put on their pure-business referral hat and leave them feeling they have been sold. You asked for a relationship.

After you ask that question, make sure to zip your lip, as silence is one of the most valuable sales techniques in the world because people hate silence and want to fill the void (plus it's super easy...you literally don't say anything). More often than not, your client/customer won't have someone in mind right then and there, so their answer will be something along the lines of *'let me give that some thought and get back to you.'* A common misconception is that this is an automatic block of the question and they are uncomfortable. This is quite the opposite. If you are genuine and sincere, your client/customer will feel that and want to reciprocate. Once that statement has been mentioned, you thank them, immediately move onto getting them on the books for your follow-up and have them on their merry way. The next time you chat, there are several ways to go about the re-ask, but always make sure you commit to your sole focus which is making sure that your existing client/customer is completely taken care of. Let's say that, during your next visit, there is a sale opportunity for your existing client/customer. There is no need to re-ask the referral question because you are already ringing your register. If, at the end of that meeting, there has not been a direct register-ringing activity, you could re-ask like this:

> *Last time we met, I remember mentioning to you that due to the growth of our business we have increased our selectivity with who we choose to serve. I know I asked this last time we spoke, but I wanted to ask who you would know that would benefit from our like-minded relationship we have? No pressure if you have not thought of anyone, as I don't want to put you on the spot!*

I happen to be a pro-humor guy (if you haven't picked up on that yet), so if you ask in a playful way, it comes across as more casual and less of a pressure sale statement. You would be shocked that, more often than not, they will have someone pop into their minds and if they mention this person's name, ask about them right then and there. Find a few nuggets of wisdom about your client's/customer's friend and, at the end, it is perfectly appropriate to ask if it would be alright for you to call them and let them know that you were sent by your client/customer. If your client/customer would prefer to reach out to them first and then make an introduction, this is equally as fine and, next time you visit, you have the ammo to ask about that person if you haven't heard back. Eventually, if you are persistent with the art of the ask (now that you have the tools to control this dance), you will land that referral. Even if you don't, your client/customer now knows to subconsciously be on the lookout for referrals to send your way because they remember the *feeling* you provide.

Before you move on to what I call the "90-day cheat code," I want to remind you that this not only works with existing clients/customers; this works exceptionally well with business partners. The main difference in this is that it's best to have already sent people your business partners' way, as there's almost the 'I owe you' syndrome that creeps into their minds. Regardless of whether you have sent people your business partners' way or not, the ask works the exact same, you just have to mold it slightly to the situation. Try something like this:

I first wanted to thank you for being such an awesome business partner, as my team and I have sincerely appreciated working with you for the greater good of our clients, not to mention it has been a load of fun getting to know you as a friend! I wanted to let you know that we are becoming more selective with who we are serving and wanted to give you a breakdown of the minimum requirements of these new clients/customers. We are looking to serve people that:

1. *Reason A*
2. *Reason B*
3. *Reason C*

With that in mind, who do you know that would benefit from the relationship and services we have provided our already-clients in common?

Unlike clients/customers, with business partners, it is ok to be a bit more black-and-white about it. This comes across as more to-the-point and with your fellow business partners, time is money for them as well, so they will appreciate it. It also plants in their minds that their best possible referrals are going to be headed your way, which in the long run is what you want, since your time will become increasingly more valuable on top of your specific career skill set becoming exponentially more efficient and effective. Your business partners are going to want to be on the same boat and so you just engrained in their brain that you want to grow *with* them and who wouldn't want to make something incredible with their friends?!

The last chapter in this section is going to be a rather brief one on the 90-day cheat code, but just because the next chapter is a quickie, that doesn't give you an automatic pass to skim through it. In the world of sales, less is more, and chapter 13 is no exception!

Chapter 13:

How to keep the good time (and referrals) rolling: the 90-day cheat code

One of the keys to success is consistency. Unless you live under a rock, this is a given. With that being said, just because it's a given doesn't mean it's not worth repeating in case you have forgotten the obvious. And when it comes to sales, this fact bears repeating over and over again.

Unlike previous chapters, we have already dipped our toe into the mastery of the ninety-day cheat code (maybe even gone in up to our knees). In this chapter, it's worth noting *why* this timeframe is mission critical and if you are in a business or industry where that frequency is simply not appropriate, you will learn how to mold it to whatever business you are working in. Far too often, it's the lack of consistency of putting the framework to use that fails my coaching clients. So you are going to learn how to control those ninety days between when you last spoke and when you're about to speak to your client/customer. This is going to set you apart from your competition.

Think back for a moment to where you left off before you and your client parted ways:

- Did you ask them who do they know?
- Who did they mention that would be interested in your services?
  - Did you connect with that person?
  - What were their interests?
  - Were you able to look them up online and learn more about them?
- Did you gather information about the business partner that your client believed would be worth getting to know?
  - Were you able to connect with them?
  - If so, what came out of that meeting?
- Was there a possible sales opportunity left open-ended from the last meeting and could happen during your next visit?

Between the last meeting and the next, these are a few of the *many* questions you need to ask yourself because the more you dig in and report back to your clients, the more your clients will have felt as though they were heard. You know how the rest of it goes: more feelings lead to more genuine connection leads to top of mind at all times, regardless of a sales situation or not.

You are probably asking why it should be ninety days. I wish I could say there have been a tremendous amount of research-backed studies on the effectiveness of this given timeframe; however, this has come not from research but from *years* of trial and error. In clients' minds, 90 days is just long enough to have a nice break from thinking about the task at hand (in terms of what you are providing them), but it's also just enough time for them not to forget about your last conversation. When you ask about a person they brought up in the last visit, or a business partner, and your client hasn't introduced you yet, chances are they will bring it up and make an effort to go through with it. If that happens, it is the perfect time to softly hold them accountable. In a circumstance like that, it would be perfectly appropriate to mention that, if you haven't heard anything by the next conversation, to go ahead and gather their information to reach out on your client's behalf. This applies to your business partners as well. If your business partner has not gone through and made an introduction that was promised, a passive, humorous guilt trip doesn't hurt the cause in terms of genuinely nudging your business partner along.

What if your client or business partner does not want to meet every ninety days OR you are in a business (like car sales), where that would simply not be appropriate? What if you have a business partner that truly does care about you and cannot meet every ninety days, but is okay with meeting every 120 (as an example)?

Answering the latter first, if you sincerely believe there is value meeting with that person, you will make sure to adjust your schedule to make time for that new-found business partner. If they have serious interest in partnering with you and only refer you every other meeting, chalk that up as a magnificent win. If I was referred a new piece of business every other meeting I had with my business partners, I would be one happy freaking camper! On the other hand, if you sense that it's one of those things where they are saying they would like to meet but their body language and eye contact are painting a different picture, even though they may *say* they have promising opportunities to send your way, take it from me when I say it is not worth your time. As Maya Angelou said, "When people show you who they are, believe them the first time." That statement has never rung more true than in the world of sales and business partnership.

Let's take a moment to go over a business where that is simply not in the cards. I mentioned car sales, but there are a TON of businesses out there where this can apply:

- HVAC companies
- Home security services
- Painters
- Builders
- Architecture
- Personal Shoppers
- Hair Stylists (if you are on my wife's schedule which is about every six months)
- Handyman
- Roofer
- Gutter cleaning
- Computer tech support

- Catering
- Wedding planning
- Photographer
- Real estate agent, residential or commercial

Just because these sales are often one-and-done, that does not mean your servicing process stops at the sale! Remember: your customers don't know the difference and if you position your servicing process as going above and beyond, they won't know the difference and will appreciate that you are doing what others are not. It would be valuable to pick a few of these examples and take you through how I would coach someone in a particular industry and what you can do to calibrate your ninety-day cheat sheet to your own business or industry.

Let's go with HVAC since it's at the top. I will use my own HVAC company as an example. They do a fantastic job and for the maintenance of our home system, they come out three times a year or so. We pay every time that the third meeting is complete and it works like clockwork. They have a recurring client in our family and the service is top-notch. This is an established brand that has been around for years and chances are they have a ton of business coming their way. A common comment I hear from businesses like this is, "We have so much business, we can hardly keep up with the demand," which is a wonderful problem to have. There are a ton of variables that go into a business like this (i.e., is there enough staff and is the staff of high quality), but those issues are beyond the scope of this book and CAPitalize Your Sales's Framework. Let's assume this business has the right number of staff in place and they are high quality, but the business is suddenly slowing down. I remember in 2022 I had a conversation with one of my longtime friends that runs a business in this industry and he had that exact issue. Business was slowed and reasons were issues that were out of his control, such as:

- The economy was slowing.
- People simply weren't thinking of their HVAC systems needing updates.
- The cost of goods to produce was skyrocketing, making it harder to turn a profit.

If you have been in a situation like this (including my buddy who I can guarantee is reading this book), then what's about to follow will save you, regardless of what economy you are in.

Let's assume the HVAC professional came out to the house, inspected it, did the initial cleaning and maintenance update, got my wife and me all squared away for the three visits a year, and booked the next meeting in four months or so. I can guarantee you the flaw is in the gap between visits. If I were coaching that company's sales reps, I would make sure to schedule a follow-up call in thirty days for ten to fifteen minutes to check in with your customers and make sure that they are still happy with what was done to their standard. Assuming that was the case and there weren't any issues, then I would close out the call with the ask you learned from chapter 12. Then, immediately after the sales maintenance rep hangs up, they would write down as much about anyone mentioned as humanly possible and during the next visit make it a priority to ask about them. After the second visit, another thirty-day follow-up, and during the third visit, there's no need to necessarily get the customer on a thirty-day call because the rep is already ringing the register with the recurring client that already trusts you and your business. If this simple process was implemented by an HVAC company, I can assure you that sales and revenue would be up by at least 20% within two years. Name me a company that wouldn't want that—there isn't one!

Let's bounce to the bottom of the list and chat about real estate agents for a moment. I must vent to you reading for a moment: there is nothing worse to me than a salesy real estate agent. Being a salesman myself, I enjoy quality salesmanship and...fun fact...people in sales are the easiest to sell to. With that being said, I would rather cut off my pinky toe than have to listen to a real estate agent ramble through all the reasons why now is the best time to buy or sell a home. Lord help us if I see these typical posts online:

> *Now's the time to buy a home, as interest rates have dropped. Give me a call.*

Or:

> *Home prices are selling at record levels. If you or someone you know is looking to sell their home, give me a call today.*

This has a guaranteed closing rate of zero...and that might be generous. Part of this could be the nature of the industry, because in order to be a successful real estate agent, you need to have a massive pipeline since some homes may not be bought or sold for three to four months. Even if this is part of the industry, I am calling BS and this is simply an excuse for the fact that agents need to up their salesmanship. This is how I would CAPitalize Your Sales if you were an agent coming to me.

Get the assumptions out of the way that you have followed the framework to a T in networking, understanding your customer's needs, getting your customers into a home and/or selling their home on the market, and that the dust has settled from the sale. When one moves (whether a home or business), it takes roughly a month or so to settle into the new normal. Knowing that, I would relay to the customer that you would love to check in with them in forty-five days to see how things are going, knowing that in the end, you will utilize the art of the genuine ask. At the end of that meeting, let the customer know that you will be checking in with them in three, six, nine months and at the year mark for ten or fifteen minutes. If your customer needs remodeling, refinancing, architectural advice or handyman work (to name a few), these are the questions that you are going to ask during those check-ins and, if your customer needs it, you have your team send it pronto. Once a year, you visit with your customers and consistently gain feedback on everything about their home. You repeat this consistently and what will happen is your customers become clients (and yes, there is a difference). I cannot tell you how many times I have spoken to real estate agents and they mention that their *clients* did XYZ and I ask them to tell me about their *clients* and they basically know their name and what their last home sold for. By turning a transaction into a recurring serviceable relationship, your sales and referrals will blast off into financial orbit. Plus, nobody will feel like they need to take a bath after talking to you.

The last example I will pick before we move onto the next section (which is going to bring in the BIG bucks) is wedding planning. Coming from the perspective of a married man, I can tell you first hand that wedding planners are NOT cheap (heck, weddings in general aren't cheap!). At the same time, while at networking events early in my career, I cannot tell you how many wedding planners I met who were getting their feet wet in the industry and, although had the most sincere of intentions, they fizzled out. What's interesting to me is that, the odds are actually in the wedding planner's favor. Most wedding planners are women and let's face it: women are better listeners than men (both in sales and life in general...ask my wife, she'd agree with me!). I say this because you ladies reading this book already have an immense upper hand over the dudes. Where men tend to push ahead is most of them are pretty aggressive in the sales process, but that's beside the point: the point I am making is that wedding planners don't need to become more sincere or aggressive in their sales process...they just need a sales process in the first place! If I were a wedding planner (which for those who know me could very well be my all-time worst nightmare), this is how I would approach it.

Using the same assumptions as before, at the end of the wedding the expectations are set. After your couple's honeymoon, set up a time a week or so after the couple returns. This gives you an easy layup in regards to what to ask the client: unless it was the honeymoon from hell, who isn't going to be excited to talk about their honeymoon?! With your couple on cloud nine, the referrals and sales are ripe for the picking. I would coordinate this meeting to have the photographer there as well and make sure to quarterback this get-together. Go over what they loved about their wedding the most and also ask what you could do to further improve, as it's a common misconception to *not* ask this question for feedback, when in reality, it is one of the most vulnerably sincere things you can present to customers or clients. As the meeting is winding down, I would ask what major events they have coming up (birthdays, holiday parties, Fourth of July, etc.) and ask what their plans are for these occasions. This is the perfect time to slip in that you plan these events as well, as the subtle hint will plant in your couple's minds that you are more than just a wedding planner (diversification is not a bad thing when used appropriately and strategically!). I would also ask if they have any other weddings they are going to in the future and, before you set up a time to check in with them in six months or so to gain further feedback about their wedding experience, close with the ask of who they would know that would benefit from the relationship similar to what you all created during the journey through their special day. Schedule the next visit, note their friends' name in your brain (and on paper if need be), and move on to the next one.

    Whatever your industry is, obviously understand the operational flow of things, but always...*always* go above and beyond by putting on your sales hat. When you play your cards right, sales to you is a service to clients/customers. Lastly, it goes without saying...but because some of you may miss it...I can't not say this enough: if there is a possible sale at the end of the meeting and it's well in advance of the next visit, make a meeting at that sales time as well as keeping up with your flow of recurring visits. At the end of the day, this is CAPitalize Your Sales and if someone says (indirectly), *"Hey I need XYZ done in a month (meaning a sale for YOU),"* don't wait until the next recurring visit. If you do that, I will disown you.

These past few sections of the book have been all about what makes you the best sales expert you can be, but eventually, you will have so much opportunity that it will come time for you to get highly selective with who you serve and continuously grow to heights and levels even about your fellow CAPitalizers. To say it another way (which is a perfect segue way into the final section of this book):

Now that you've made it, become the best of the best.

SECTION 4:

Now that you've made it, become the best of the best.

Before you move on to the final section of this book, it's worth your time to take a moment and truly appreciate how far you have come (and how fast you have done so!). One of my greatest mistakes has been not being able to appreciate accomplishments that make it across the finish line and if I could go back and redo things, that would be one of my main regrets. I want you to *profoundly* take in everything you have learned and I can guarantee that you have become a better man or woman since you started this journey.

Another point I want to make is that some of you will tell yourselves that the first three sections of this book are all that you need to succeed in **CAPitalizing Your Sales**. If you are earning what you need to not only live, but be happy and live abundantly, no judgement here and good for you for knowing your level of happiness (unfortunately, there is no '75% off' button for this book, but hey...nothing is perfect!). In all seriousness, it takes a true man or woman to know where to draw the line and, in many ways, I wish I could have that ability. After reading these first three sections and mastering the framework for several years, it would not shock me in the slightest if you are making six figures, regardless of your career. When I say six figures, I am talking *easily* $100,000, $200,000, and if you are seasoned with the framework and have been at it for years, the tune of $500,000+ is not out of the question. Making hundreds of thousands of dollars is beyond impressive and I will never take away from anyone making any living, period, especially those who have cracked that code that this book has laid out.

Sections 1-3 will make you hundreds of thousands; Section 4 will make you millions.

Eventually, there will come a point where you are going to have to decide whether to keep hitting the grindstone OR realize it is more of a financial gain to simply focus on your existing client/customer base. This is where you will have to transform from a sales expert to a CEO of your career or business, which is what Chapter 14 will be all about. With rare exceptions, when you reach this moment in your career, if you want to take that monumental leap, one of the most valuable practices you will implement is learning what task or tasks bring you the most money. Can you get out of *everything* else? Probably not (although...if you can...call me because I can learn from YOU!). There are, however, a number of tasks that are simply not worth your time and/or are not your strong suit and learning the power of outsourcing is the name of the game when it comes to Chapter 15. Not only will you learn the power of outsourcing conceptually from a time-freeing standpoint; you will also learn the business side as to the net cost benefit to your bottom line. Saying it another way: it takes money to make money and you will see the reasons why you need to know this saying inside and out. Regardless of if you stopped after section 3 to put your *CAPitalize Your Sales Framework* on cruise control or kept on truckin' with Chapter 14 and 15, the final chapter in this section will teach you something that not a single sales "coach" or "guru" mentions: there will come a point where it does not make financial or business sense to reinvest back into your sales framework. Where do you go with that money? Simple: start reinvesting into yourself. My followers have heard me say this many times on our podcast and it bears worth repeating: *the best investment you can guarantee is an investment in yourself.* For the first several years of mastering the *CAPitalize Your Sales Framework*, you will keep reinvesting everything back into you, which is the smart thing to do. After a while, you will notice that there simply may not be anywhere else in your framework to reinvest your hard-earned profits from your sales efforts, and this is where you can begin prudently taking your money and start making intelligent investment decisions. Chances are that someday you will want to transition out of what you are currently doing or retire, and you are going to want to maintain the standard of living you have worked so hard for. Unfortunately, if you have not invested outside of your framework, unless you own a business that you are planning on selling, you'll be out of luck. Knowing what you need to do financially is where my book, *CAPitalize Your Finances*, comes into play, but this chapter will give you a 50,000-foot view of how you need to think about taking your hard-earned profits and diversifying outside of yourself.

Now that you know what is coming down the home stretch, get ready to add a zero to your income.

It's time to become the best of the best.

Chapter 14:
Transform from sales expert to CEO

You may not believe me when I say this: someday you will no longer have the issue of garnering new sales opportunities. I mentioned in the intro to this section that sticking to your existing clients will be more valuable than going out and constantly hunting for new ones. This transformation from sales expert to CEO is critical if you are looking to add another zero to your income.

There is a rule in business called the '80/20' rule. This means 80% of your business or sales comes from 20% of your clients. After years of growing your business or your brand, you are going to quickly realize that your situation is no different. So why bother looking anywhere else when you can tap into your "twenty-percenters" to surround yourself with more of them?! This may seem like common sense, but to implement this needs further explanation, as it is *not* cut and dried.

As of now, you know the value of the ninety-day cheat code and of systematically meeting with clients, customers, and business partners to both maintain an amazing relationship and pick up referral possibilities in the process. There will come a time, however, when you are so slammed that time is non-existent. If you have gotten to that place, the big question is: *now what?*

Most sales coaches and gurus discuss separating clients/customers into different categories like A, B, and C. This is foolish because when you are starting off, that should NOT be the main focus. What your primary focus should be is gaining as many sales opportunities as possible and building quality relationships with everyone who sets foot in your place of work. If you attempt to do this too early, you will take your eye off the greatest value that is your goodwill. That will decimate your reputation and you will become no different than any other sleazeball of a salesman.

Going back two paragraphs, when the time comes when you are *truly* that slammed (or can see that time coming up rapidly), **that** is the time where utilizing the classic A, B and C segmentation comes into play. Despite what you may think, it's actually **not** making some clients/customers more or less important than others, and everyone will appreciate it. Let's think about this for a second:

Pretend that every client/customer meets with you on a regular ninety-day schedule. After years of perfecting your craft and gaining a ton of business (as well as perfecting this framework to a T), your calendar is blocked. You have hit your capacity. This is what I would do in this case.

You first want to ask yourself if any of your clients/customers truly need to meet this frequently. Some inevitably still will, but others will only need to meet twice or once a year. Make a list of your clients/customers and mark which ones need to meet less frequently. Once you do that, mark it in your calendar to let them know during the next visit and, after that get-together, get them on their new schedule.

A common question I get asked by coaching clients is: will they be upset or offended? Not if you position it accordingly, and sometimes there is not even a need to position it because it's common sense. I can give you a couple examples from my business, and my clients are not mad, upset, or negative in any way.

We have one retired client who needs $4,000 a month to live comfortably. From her social security, two pensions, and an annuity, she receives $5,000 a month. Without talking about *anything else* from her portfolio, she is *making* $1,000 a month. Because of this, we meet with her on an annual basis and she is perfectly fine with it because we are still treating her with amazing service and she knows her situation is now in a realm of ultra-simplicity, which actually puts her more at ease than when we met quarterly before she retired. Everyone wins, as she frees up hours of her time every year and I free up a ton of my time to further grow my business, help more people, and earn a higher revenue per unit of time. Again, this chapter is about transforming from a sales expert to a CEO. This is the type of stuff the big boys think about (and so should you!).

Another client who we have had for a while retired with a similar circumstance as the prior one, but is a bit anxious about easing into that next chapter of their life. They still would like to meet more than once a year, but understood that twice a year would be optimal for the time being after I positioned it accordingly. Saying something like this would make the clients feel better and know it's simply part of my process:

> Mr. And Mrs. Client, we are super-excited that you have made it to the promised land of retirement! Because your monthly income is not only met, but guaranteed, we are going to change our quarterly meetings to a semi-annual schedule. That way, you can enjoy your retirement to the fullest and save you time meeting with us throughout the year! On top of that, now that you are retired, the movement within your portfolio and timing certain events (such as you retiring) are set in stone and because you are absolutely golden, we will be meeting semi-annually going forward to make sure you are all systems go and simply check in on you. You have done all the hard work and it's time you go out and enjoy it!!!

You never....*never* want people to feel as though they are lessor/not worth it anymore, etc., because that is not the case! If your client/customer is all set and not needing as much from you, you are actually showing how much you care about them. Once you go through and free up your calendar with this simple exercise, you will quickly realize that you just freed up a TON of time to further rev your sales engine. The best part: since you know how to elegantly ask, that calendar will fill right back up, only this time you are making *even MORE money*.

Before you learn about the power of outsourcing, it's worth your time to learn how to attack this role as a CEO with business partners. It is inevitable that someday you will have partners that simply stop referring to you or slow down significantly. Only you will be able to read the situation to see if it is sincerely worth your time continuing down that path. If not, don't simply ghost them and leave them high and dry. Just be honest. Say something like this:

> *[Business Partner], I wanted to chat with you about our quarterly get-togethers. I am simply buried with work and want to keep getting together, but I don't know if I can continue this frequency. Would it be all right if we cut it back to [three times a year, twice or once a year depending on the circumstance] or could we put it on hold and once things slow down, I can reach out and get us back on the recurring bandwagon?*

That way, no bridges were burned (as you are sincerely more and more busy), and the door is always left open.

A final nugget I will leave you with in this chapter is to think of this from the numbers side of things. Let's say you had the following client/customer breakdown and revenue earned annually per person:

- 20 A's earning you $100,000 total (so $5,000 per year or $1,250 per visit).
- 40 B's earning you $100,000 total (so $2,500 per year or $625 per visit).
- 30 C's earning you $50,000 total (so $1,666.67 per year or $416.66 per visit).

If you took the C's and met with them only once a year, your sale per visit would shoot up from $416.66 to $1,666.67 which is an increase of 4x. Not only that, you just freed up ninety hours a year of purely meeting with these people (if we assume each meeting lasts one hour). This doesn't include the work you do between get-togethers...so call it 180 hours if every meeting requires another hour of administrative tasks. If you are working 2,000 hours a year, simply by reducing contact with your C's (but still providing quality service), you just added 9% of your time back which could, all things being equal, add an additional 9% back to your annual sales income. That's just with the C's!

Speaking of numbers, in the next chapter, you will learn the power of outsourcing and further your comprehension of becoming the CEO of *CAPitalizing Your Sales* Framework. Who knew this would transition into a comprehensive business advice book??? (Other than me, I guess...).

Chapter 15:

Learn the power of outsourcing

Those who know me know I jokingly love to say that I am a master at outsourcing. It's true...I am only maximally efficient at a few things. Before we discuss those tasks I excel at, for your humorous pleasure, here are a few of the many things that it would be far from ideal to hire me for in your next business endeavor:

- Administrative duties
- Plumbing
- Car servicing
- Social media marketing
- Home remodeling
- Landscaping
- Haiku poetry
- Ghost writing
- Roofing
- Electrical

As you can tell from this abbreviated list, there are many things that are not my cup of tea. Sure, there are things that I simply have zero training on (electrician), but there are also duties listed that I either knowingly suck at (social media marketing, landscaping, car servicing) or fancy to imagine that the ending would not be a happy one for our hero if he attempted these (Home remodeling: might as well bomb the home. Ghost writing: can't pretend to be someone else. Administrative duties: call my office and ask my teammate Betty...she'll laugh). As for the haiku poetry, if you haven't realized...I can be long in the tooth (hence why I need to write an entire book on topics), so a 5-7-5 syllable poem will either be purely horrendous due to my excessive explanations or (most likely) blatantly inappropriate due to my humor that parallels that of a *highly intellectual* eight-year-old boy. Where am I going with this?

Whenever I can, I outsource. *

Let's throw some serious examples of the power of outsourcing onto the page. I'm first going to use my business as an example, follow up with a few hypothetical businesses, and then finish this chapter as I always prefer to do: getting you to think.

If you are just starting out in the world of sales, regardless of where you are, the chances are that this chapter won't be as valuable at first due to a simple fact: you aren't making any money (yet) so you cannot necessarily afford to outsource any of your tasks that you know you aren't top-notch at. This is *not* a bad thing and I always....*always* coach starters in whatever industry you're in, you *need* to roll up your sleeves and dig into every aspect of your business, regardless if you own it or not. If you don't know how to coach up your next employee on assisting in certain tasks, how in the world are they going to figure them out? There is no faster way to lose trust and respect than to tell someone to do something when your people know damn well that you have never done the tasks you're dishing out OR...even worse...wouldn't do them yourself.

When I started out in my business, the first two years were absolute hell due to the fact that I had to make it happen in every aspect of the business. On top of what brought home the bacon for my business (sales and financially planning for clients), I was chief operating officer, heading up administrative tasks and filling out every lick of paperwork, driving to FedEx nearly daily to mail out original paperwork, posting social media messages and responding to everything that came my way, and even janitorial services. Even though I loved it (yes, you have to love being in hell for the first part of your career...trust me...you'll miss it), I knew that if I wanted to get married and have kiddos, there is no way on God's green earth that I could have kept up the fifteen hours a day from Monday-Friday and twelve to fourteen more on Saturdays (on top of administrative duties Sundays) and be a present father and husband. Aside from the profound love I had for my future wife and kids, the fact of the matter was that I was well aware that *nobody* can keep that schedule up forever, so even though I was not comfortably breaking even in my practice, I knew I needed help...and fast. That is when God blessed me with the best teammate I could have ever asked for in Betty!!!

People who don't know the business ask what Betty does and that would require an entirely new book just for descriptions, but to keep the big picture simple: she has mastered the tasks that she knows I am not the best at. By doing this, she knows I have more time to get out there and hit the big-ticket items that will further expand the business (and provide benefits like pay raises, bonuses, flexible schedules, and overall positivity in the workplace). To give you an idea of how the numbers pan out, let's throw some onto the page.

I never discuss compensation with anyone, as it's nobody's business other than mine and my teammates,' but let's hypothetically say that, on an hourly basis, the business would make $350 an hour. Is filling out paperwork the best use of those valuable hours for me? Nope. By understanding that and getting help, my return on investment within my business skyrockets. To make math easy, in Washington State where I live, minimum wage is about $16 an hour, so by paying that to someone to fill out paperwork, my net revenue for the business is $334. Let's also take it a step further and say that what used to take me two hours takes an employee thirty minutes. Finally, let's say that thirty minutes is how long a business sale takes, so if you completed four of those in two hours, you'd be infinitely happier (and better off financially) vs you diving headfirst into the admin. In two hours, the difference between outsourcing or not is substantial:

1. By not paying to outsource, you are bootstrapped at completing that paperwork, so sure, you are "making" the $350 an hour, but you are not able to do anything else (like go and bring in more business at that rate). Your revenue: $700.

2. Outsourcing to pay the hypothetical $16 an hour, your administrative expert is now paid $32 over that two-hour span. On the other hand, you can close four...*four* new sales at that $350 rate, so that results in $1,400 - $32 = $1,368 total revenue in that span.

With everything, there is a balancing act, but the hypothetical situation is clear in the fact that, if you are trying to crush it, outsourcing had better become your middle name.

Let's move on to real estate sales. This one is pretty black and white: as an agent, you get paid on sales of homes, lands or apartments. The larger the deals, the smaller the percentage, but to keep it simple, assume the average commission is 6%, with 3% going to the buying agent and 3% going to the selling agent. Going further, let's say that the average home sale price is $412,000.[9] If you sell one home a month, that's $12,360 (3% of either agent side) x 12 months = $148,320 a year. Imagine if you hired someone to complete the paperwork, call inspectors, and follow up with customers on potential offers. For most real estate agents, the sale (although *the* largest and only revenue provider) often takes the shortest amount of time. Going with the hypothetical, if you are closing on a home every month, let's assume a full week of the month is devoted to the actual sales side of things (going to homes, chatting with customers to compare homes, and finalizing a deal). The three weeks dedicated to the things *not* bringing in business are deadly in terms of growth, so if you hired a full timer at $60,000 (pay and benefits), you could free up three weeks of your month and potentially close on a home a *week*. If that was the case, here are two scenarios for you to chomp on:

1. No outsource: $148,320 a year.
2. Outsource: pay $60,000 a year for ancillary duties to make $593,280, netting $533,280 a year.

I have had people in the industry balk at this example, saying it doesn't work like that, so let's assume this example is off by 50%...you'd still net $236,640 a year vs. $148,320. Without diving into nerdiness on the actual return on investment, it's a no freaking brainer to pay someone 'x' to potentially earn two to four times 'x.'

Unless you genuinely struggle with the concept of putting two and two together, you have most likely come to realize that outsourcing is one of the simplest, yet most valuable tools you need to have in your toolkit if you are trying to add a zero onto your annual sales goal. With that being said, every industry is different and unless you or your boss is paying me to come out and dive into your business specifically, only you are going to know what is most valuable. Because of this, I have a task for you to complete.

Take out a sheet of paper and write down what you made in the prior year. Once you have that down, write down all of the tasks that you either knowingly suck at and/or tasks that you know are least valuable in terms of growing your business or sales goal. After you do this, look up what a going rate would be for someone that fits this new-found job description and if there is affordability for you to bring on this person, you know the next step: use the techniques you have learned in this book to ask your friends, family, customers, or clients and business partners to see who they know that would be a wonderful fit for your team! While you're finding this person, go through one more exercise to see what you would earn if you outsourced to your newbie and freed up time to ring your register more frequently. Not only will this get you fired up, you will also learn what the most successful business owners, CEOs and CFOs out there do on a daily basis to become the best of the best.

You will do this again and again...and again, as the best investment out there is in yourself. As much as I love this concept, unfortunately...I hate to say this (I *really* do)...that reinvestment will eventually become a *poor* investment and you will need to learn to pivot that profit. On top of that, eventually most people want to retire at some point in time and unless you run a business that you could possibly sell down the road, you are going to need to stop reinvesting into your sales framework and start investing *outside* of yourself.

This brings us to the final chapter in the framework, my friends!!!

*Minus haikus. I skip out on haikus altogether.

Chapter 16:

When it's time to *stop* reinvesting into your framework (and instead invest in yourself)

A s you read in the previous chapter, the best investment you can make is in yourself. Most influencers say that and simply leave it as is, but now that you have the previous chapter in your back pocket, you can quantifiably back that statement with monetary facts. The greatest business minds out there would gladly take a dollar to earn it back in three years, as that would be a 33% return on your money (in the world of business, we call that return on invested capital, or ROIC for short). Whether you are a sales rep at a company, a small business owner, or Tim Cook, the CEO of Apple, you now understand one of the greatest concepts in terms of making more money. The greatest businesses out there know that if they can earn substantially higher rates of return on growing the business by reinvesting back into it, they are going to do so without hesitation. There is a catch to this:

> *Like all great things,*
> *efficient ROIC will someday come to a halt.*

Keeping with the 33% example from above, if you can keep on doing that for years, especially if you run a business, do so. All businesses have a plateau at some point, so let's say that your ROIC is not 33%, but instead dwindling to a "mere" 25% (I am being sarcastic, of course). Do you still reinvest within the business? Absolutely. There is one question that you will need to answer, which is when do you stop reinvesting within your framework or business and start taking those profits to reinvest *outside* of what got you where you are today?

This is not a black-and-white answer, but I will give you guardrails to get you to think about that moment, as it will come faster than you may realize. Let's say that your business/sales naturally grow at 15% a year without you reinvesting anything back into the process. Is that a 15% ROIC? *No*...it's just the natural 15% growth in your process, regardless of whether you reinvest or not. Does it make sense to take profits to reinvest back into your framework? It comes down to this: what is the return? If there is no ROIC (or, heaven forbid, a negative return), instead of reinvesting, distributing those profits to you and your family to begin to invest in assets outside of your framework will be the name of the game.

What if you don't have anything saved up for retirement and you are a salesperson at your company? Even though you can reinvest within your framework and earn an ungodly rate of return, it is meaningless in the fact that, when you move on or retire, you take....you guessed it....*zero* of that with you. This is when you need to take your profits and begin to diversify outside of your framework so that someday, you can transition or retire on *your* terms.

By no means is this going to get into the weeds of financial planning or investing, as my first book, *CAPitalize Your Finances*, is dedicated to this topic in *great* detail. The point I am getting at is that you need to think about how you are going to be able to ride off into the sunset, and the balancing act of reinvesting within your framework vs investing in investments that will make money for you is an overlooked, yet extraordinarily valuable question that sales coaches never...and I mean *never* ask their students.

For now, I will simply ask you to complete the following, as it's a fantastic 50,000-foot view of whether you can move on from what you are doing and be able to afford your current lifestyle. This also assumes you don't own a business (which I will cover after this).

Take a moment to write down your monthly expenses. Whatever they are, know that your expenses today will not be your expenses tomorrow, so you need to account for inflation at the time you are planning on retiring altogether. What I recommend for my clients is to think about inflation growing historically at 2.5% annually per year, so inflate that number of monthly expenses by 2.5% from today until the time you will retire (so however many years that is). Once you have done that, multiply that number by twelve to get an annual expense need and divide that number by 4%. This is by no means a perfect number, but in my line of work, there is a general rule of thumb that if you take 4% of your portfolio to live on within retirement, there is a solid chance your money will outlive you (not 100%, but a good chance nonetheless). Whatever that lump sum is happens to be the number you will need to have saved up at that point of pulling the plug for retirement. If you have zero clue how to get there, that's where *CAPitalize Your Finances* comes into play, as it's one thing to make a ton of money; it's a whole other thing to become a steward of your earnings. You will need to learn how to balance reinvesting within your framework and investing outside of your framework, and that topic is beyond the scope of this book.

If you run a business, you have a massive advantage in that, more likely than not, you have something you can sell to a potential buyer. If that is the case, everything you read in the paragraph above still applies, with one addition: you need to understand what the value of your business is. Businesses are sold based on a multiple of either revenue, net income (profit) or EBITDA (Earnings before interest, taxes, depreciation and amortization), but in terms of what your specific business will be valued at, it is much more complicated than that. It would be well worth your time to understand the value of your business today as well as unlocking the potential value you are missing out on to maximize the sale of your business. The book I would read is *The Business Transition Handbook* by my dear friend and business partner Laurie Barkman. On her website, there is a tool that you can use to get a better understanding of what your business can *truly* be sold for and having someone like Laurie in your back pocket to further grow that ROIC will lead you to the ultimate sale of your lifetime. Here is the link to her book:

https://thebusinesstransitionsherpa.com/the-business-transition-handbook/[10]

By no means does the conclusion of this book in this chapter need to be something of a morbid thought: far from it. After all, whether you know it or not, you are no longer thinking merely as a sales pro; you are thinking as the CEO of your business and/or brand. By going through these processes, you will have a couple things happen to you:

1. You will learn what you will need to have to live comfortably long after you are done selling in your respective field.
2. You will learn how to work backwards and start to shift hard-earned profits from all-in on your framework to balancing how much to invest in assets that will work for you both now and into the future so that you can retire on your terms.
3. You will overcome the fear of the unknown that nearly 100% of sales professionals (as well as people in general) simply have zero clue about: "How much do I need in retirement and how to get there?"
4. Due to that huge question no longer being an issue, you will be able to continuously sell with infinitely less stress, which will naturally compound your sales numbers even higher than before!

To put it another way: with less stress, you'll sell more genuinely and the more genuine and sincere you are, the more you sell. It's that simple.

Chapter 17:
Why am I doing this?

Before we conclude this book with some tools to help you achieve the *CAPitalize Your Sales Framework*, it is worth first mentioning that...uh, helllloooooo....CONGRATULATIONS! You now have the tools, skills and strategies to take your income and double, triple, quadruple...heck...the sky is the limit, my friend. You are probably wondering why I am choosing to end this book with this chapter now that you have everything at your fingertips to get out there and make a name for yourself in the name of genuine and sincere sales mastery. The truth is that this chapter has nothing to do with sales; it has to do with life.

When I started in the world of business, I admittedly was drawn to all of the wrong things. It's totally acceptable to have money goals, *especially* when you have no money to speak of, and it's valuable to set high bars and standards for yourself year after year. I say this because, in the beginning, I was *unknow-*

ingly drawn to "the next dollar," and, after your needs and your family's needs are met, there is a brief period of elevated happiness, but it evaporates in an instant. You have all read my business's numbers. Was there an increased level of happiness when I broke even? You betcha! Unfortunately, it took me a couple years *after* I broke even to recognize that it had absolutely *zero* to do with the money from that point on. I don't have many regrets in my life, but one of the big ones is I wish I could go back and tell myself what I am about to tell you now...

Everyone has a gift worth sharing with the world. Sure, some of us have more gifts than others, but we all have at least **one**. For example, my brother Tyler has one of, if not *the*, greatest social media minds I have ever tapped into. My dear friend Nick Hutchison has the ability to succinctly connect with anyone in an instant. One of my past guests and my idol-turned-colleague, William Green, is quite possibly the best I have ever witnessed at asking questions. For those that watch football, Alec Ingold is known on the field as one of the best fullbacks around; off the field, I have gotten to know him on a personal level and he has an ability to exert what I would call "concentrated love" more efficiently than just about anyone on planet earth. Lastly (but *certainly not* least), Kristen Butler's gift of finding ways to help others is one of a kind, as she doesn't even have to say she is going to do something because the next thing you know, you've been helped.

Why am I bringing up all of these gifts? As a podcast host, I have had the privilege and blessing of interviewing some of the greatest business, entrepreneurial, investing, and overall money minds of all time. After a few years in, I came to realize something in common with those that I had interviewed that were... shall we say..."closer to the checkout line" in life. Offline, I like to learn about those who are older and wiser than me, specifically if they have any regrets in life. In a multitude of variations, the common regret is that they wish they could start giving their gifts back to society sooner.

How many people go through their entire life and die with everything they learned? Think about how selfish and sad that is. I'd put money on the fact that most multi-millionaires and billionaires will go out and pass along nothing in terms of life lessons and gifts they were blessed with.

Back in 2021, I came to the realization that I could have easily focused solely on my business, compounded my business at the rate of 18% or so and become every other top financial planner in the country: financially fat and happy. If I did that, there was a zero percent chance I would have looked back on my life and said that was the right thing to do. Would it have been the most prudent thing for my *career*? Sure, and coming from a guy who gets paid to financially plan for some of the most successful business owners, executives and athletes on the planet, that is the advice I would give myself if I asked what would be the most optimal thing from a business perspective. There is one problem with that:

There is plenty of life after your sales career or business.

Being a man of faith, I am a big believer in the fact that, someday, we will all have to answer for our actions. Knowing the regrets of those I look up to, I am fortunate to still (hopefully) have a ton of runway left where I can not only compound my family's good fortune and my clients' financial success; I can also compound my giving of my gifts. When I hit those pearly gates, I want to be able to look The Big Man in the eyes, thank Him for my wonderful life and tell Him that, to the absolute best of my abilities, I gave it everything. I kept my body as healthy as I could, did my best to be a present father and husband, took care of my family, friends and clients, was a steward of His gifts He blessed me with, and gave back as much as possible.

I want to leave you with a thought. Ask yourself why you are doing this? Sure, we started this book with the construction of your purpose, but take it deeper. Do your absolute best to try to reverse engineer your life. What do you want to be remembered for? Where to you want to get in life? Who are you going to surround yourself with and what qualities do these people possess? Most importantly, what are your gifts? If you believe in God like I do, what are those God-given gifts and how are you going to bless them upon all the people in your life? If you don't, that's ok too! Whatever you believe, ask the equivalent.

Regardless of what you do, always ask yourself why you are doing what you do. Sure, there can be surface-level immediate desires, such as, "I want to pay off my student loan," or, "I want to lose fifteen pounds of stubborn body fat," but those will only get you so far. The deeper you dig, the greater you will feel, and once you dig so far that you can't possibly dig any deeper, you have found exactly why you are doing what you are doing and, once you do, do not ever...*ever* stop reaching for it.

Thank you so much for picking up a copy of **CAPitalize Your Sales** and if you ever have any questions about your framework, feel free to follow me on Instagram (capincapitalize), X (@CAPinCAPitalize) or LinkedIn (Christopher Panagiotu). If you run a business or sales division of your company and would like your team to learn how to *CAPitalize* their Sales Process, feel free to send my team a message by either going to https://capitalizepodcast.com/ or emailing my social media manager tyler@vitalmediastudios.com to have me and my team come out to teach you and your people how to *CAPitalize Your Sales and CAPitalize Your Finances.*

My only ask is that, if you found this book helpful, please give it a proper five-star review from wherever you purchased it and share the *CAPitalized word* with your friends, family and business partners.

No more feeling sleazy, conniving, or overall negative in any sales situation. My prayer is that you found this extraordinarily helpful and are well on your way to growing your business and/or brand to the fullest with the heart of a genuine and sincere sales master. Go with that message and...as I tell all my listeners, followers, clients and colleagues...

Keep *CAPitalizing,*

Christopher A Panagiotu, The *CAP* in *CAPitalize*

Tools to keep you on track in CAPitalizing Your Sales

Client/ Prospect	Initial Contact	Appointment	Initial Meeting	Closing Meeting

Sale	Dollar Amount	One Time Sale or Reoccurring	Referral?

Now that you have read through CAPitalize Your Sales in its entirety, it's time for you to get out there and get to CAPitalizing immediately! In order for you to successfully CAPitalize You Sales, you are going to need a template for you to keep track of what is going on with your sales process. In this chapter, I am giving you the exact template I used when I first started to get REALLY serious about my sales process and the best part about it is you will quickly recognize that, despite this process being incredibly simple to follow, it's immensely valuable and in 3 seconds, you will be able to figure out *exactly* where you need to improve your sales game. I want to briefly touch on every column and then you are truly ready to rock and roll!

Anytime I met with a client or prospect, I would write down their names. It's pretty obvious that this goes in the client/prospect column, but what isn't obvious is how valuable this column can be. If you are trying to grow your business and/or earn more sales from new clients/customers and all you are doing is meeting with current clients/customers, this is a glaring sign that you need to roll up your sleeves and get back out there to spread the word about your brilliance! What I would do is write either a "c" or a "p" next to each person's name and at the end of every week, I would review who and what I am meeting with the most. If you are meeting with a business partner or potential business partner, I would mix it up slightly. With existing business partners, simply putting a "b" next to their name should suffice. With possible newbies to your professional circle of friendship, you could put either a "b" or a "p", as I could make the argument that every new person you come in contact with is a prospect.

I would check off the initial meeting box if it was...well... an initial interaction of course! Most of the time prospects and initial contact coincide; however, there are times where you could argue that the initial time meeting a prospect was simply getting them on the calendar to have an official initial chat, so if that was the case, I would be fine if there wasn't a checked box next to their name.

The appointment box is checked when you get prospects/clients to commit to coming into your office, place of work or getting on a call for that initial meeting OR closing meeting. This is where the process starts to come alive because you can quickly decipher where your process is falling apart, quickly go back into this book, reread what chapter is most important and then implement to fill in the sales gap. Let's say that you have a ton of initial contacts lined up but your appointments of getting these people in the door to sit and start your process is basically empty. That tells me as a sales coach that you need to work on the transition to making sure these potential sales actually make it into your respective place of work to truly get to know what you provide, your process and have a successful initial meeting.

The initial meeting is another fairly obvious box. If it is the first time you are meeting with a prospect to get the party started, that is where you mark this column off. If you have an existing client where you are presenting a new strategy or arm of your business where you could make a new type of sale with that existing client, I would qualify that as an initial meeting as well. Even though these people already work with you, you are introducing them to a new service which is almost like a new client experience all together.

The closing meeting is the fun stuff. These are marked when your prospect/client is coming back into your place of work to potentially ring your register. Not only is this the most exciting meeting; this is the most important piece of the process and will slap you in the face if you are NOT closing. Let's say you are marking off boxes left and right; meeting/calling prospects, nailing the initial contact, committing them to appointments, knocking it out of the park with initial meetings and moving them on to your closing meetings...BUT no sales. This took me a few years to really dial in, but the good news is that, after a few years of figuring this out on my own, I can tell you this is BY FAR the easiest boat to turn around if you are the metaphorical Titanic headed for the iceberg that is the sales graveyard. Chapter 8 will quickly become your best friend.

A common question I get from business clients and sales professionals I coach is what's the point of the sale, dollar amount, one time sale or reoccurring columns? Their reasoning is a sale is a sale, so I should be proud of them and they are ragingly hyped for putting money in their pockets. If you are *just* starting out, I wouldn't read *too* much into these columns, as for newbies, that reasoning is 100% correct. If you are broker than broke, any sale is a win and regardless of the dollar amount or if it is a reoccurring sale, etc., the point is it's a sale. Overtime, these columns become immensely more valuable as you start to transition from a simple sales pro to a CEO of your life. You will get to a point where you can sell to anyone, but that is a long term issue. As you get better at what you do, your time will become immensely more valuable and so the dollar amount column starts to play an immensely larger role of importance.

It doesn't matter if you are a CPA, HVAC specialist, Plumber, Painter, Real estate agent, etc. You are going to want to make sure that dollar amount per sale increases overtime. Let's work backwards: say you want to make $1,000,000 in a year. Let's also say you work 48 weeks a year due to holidays/birthdays/time to recharge/etc. $1,000,000 / 48 weeks is $20,833.33 per week. Assuming you want to work 40 hours a week, $20,833.33 per week / 40 hours means you have to earn $520.83 an hour. Once you know what you want to make and do the same respective calculation, then go back to your worksheet and look at the dollar amount per sale. In this case, if you are having closing meetings that take an hour and you are making $520.83 per sale, you are on track for your goal. If not, that's when you start to look into your book of clients/business partners and start to implement minimums that will get you to that goal. You may think this will slow down your sales process…that is incredibly false. From my experience, the more my practice's minimum is raised, the more referrals come in the door…it's insane! The famous Psychologist and lecturer Jordan Peterson refers to this concept as Price's Law, which states that as you become better at your craft, more people want to work with you, so by definition you have the right to get more and more picky because the law mathematically states that you don't have to worry! In terms of if a sale is a one time sale or reoccurring, this is where it gets very interesting. Depending on the industry, I have clients that make the argument that all of their sales are one timers. Car sales, painters, architects to name a few. The argument is simple: once you sell a car, it will be a while until you buy another. Once you paint your house, it probably won't need another paint job. Once a building is built...it's built! I see the reasoning but respectively disagree with all of it and can prove it to you. If you simply want to peak as a sales pro and not convert to a CEO of your life, by all means go for it. Also if you enjoy the thrill of that hunt, that's perfectly fine! Most of you; however, want to consistently level up in CAPitalizing Your Sales, so if that is the case, convert your one timers and make them reoccurring sales. Car sales: if the customer leased the car, you know they have to come in at the end of the lease. If it's a 3 year lease (as an example), set a follow up call 90 days after the initial lease and go through what I have taught you. Then, depending on your level of activity in the dealership, setup another time to chat in 90 or 180 days and continue to do so until their lease comes up for renewal. During those meetings, consistently ask who they know at the end of every call/interaction. Your car sales will skyrocket. As for painting or architecture, make it your own! Follow up after the project is complete in 90 days. After that, check in 180 days or even a year after and go through the same process. It doesn't have to be a ton of time either...we are talking about 30 minutes max. If you gain a referral from these calls, you are golden and in those respective industries, it doesn't have to be a high close rate...even if it's a referral rate of 5-10%, you are going to be beyond happy and give it a few years that number compounds to the moon!

    The last column is the referral column. You are going to want to mark this off if during *any* interaction, there is some mention of a referral, whether you directly asked or the prospect/client mentions someone or a business that would be in need of your services, directly or indirectly. A tip I want to throw out: if you are closing a new piece of business and land the sale, I wouldn't ask for a referral...focus on the sale in front of you, plus people can feel when they are being used as a stepping stone to 'the next sale' and you never want anyone to feel that way with you. If there is not a direct sale during your interactions with clients, end the interaction with the 'who do you know?' technique you learned in this book. If you are wanting more referrals but are simply not getting any, this column will be key because if you are asking (you could put a "ask" in the column) but not receiving any, that tells you that you need to improve the art of the ask. It's worth mentioning that, most of the time, the first ask clients won't have someone on the top of mind and that is totally fine. Your initial ask is the planting of the seed! After a few times chatting with them and asking in different ways, if they simply don't have anyone but are great clients, stop asking, as it will come off as pushy. Plus, if someone does ask who your client knows that does what you do, what will happen is pure magic: because you planted that seed, the client will blossom that seed immediately into sending more referrals your way. It's a beautiful thing! Another point worth knowing: the larger the sale, the longer it takes to gain referrals. In my line of work as a Certified Financial Planner, there have been times where I have worked with clients for as long as 7 years and then suddenly, referrals start flooding in from them. Be patient and the referrals will begin to flow, but stay on top of this last column to make sure the icing on the cake of your CAPitalize Your Sales process is picture perfect.

Acknowledgments

This book would not have been possible without the support, guidance, and encouragement of several extraordinary individuals.

First and foremost, I want to express my deepest gratitude to my wife, Stephanie. Your unwavering support, patience, and love have been my rock throughout this process. Your belief in me, even during the most challenging times, has been a source of strength and inspiration. Thank you for always standing by my side and for your constant encouragement. I love you more than you will ever know (although I am pretty sure you have a good idea!)

How can I not acknowledge my sweet baby girl, Abigail?! Your presence in my life brings immeasurable joy and motivation. I hope that as life progresses, you can use this book (as well as my other one) to jumpstart your life's successes and your Mom and I are always giving our all to make sure you continue to be the happiest little girl in the world. Thank you for your endless hugs, smiles, and for being a constant source of light and happiness. You're our little angel!

I am also deeply grateful to my amazing mom, Julie. Your unconditional love and support have been instrumental in shaping who I am today. Your wisdom, guidance, and encouragement have been invaluable throughout this process. Thank you for always believing in me and for being my biggest cheerleader, as well as putting up with me all these years!

To my brother and social media manager, Tyler. Your hard work and dedication have been crucial in reaching and engaging with our audience. Your creativity and strategic thinking have been invaluable. Thank you for your commitment and for always going above and beyond. It takes a special person to keep me in my lanes and I would want no other person helping grow The CAPitalize Movement than you! We are just getting started and it will be a tremendous blessing to see what the future holds for the brand and know that without you, none of this would have been possible!

A special thank you to my publisher, Morgan James. Your belief in my work and your support throughout the publishing process have been immensely appreciated. Thank you for your professionalism, guidance, and for helping bring this project to fruition.

To my AMAZING assistant and teammate, Betty. Holy smokes, where do I even begin?! As I mentioned earlier in Ty's acknowledgement, it takes a special person to work alongside yours truly and our (nearly) eight years together have been a rollercoaster of…well…everything! Brutal lows, SUPER highs and everything in between. Best of all, I got to enjoy these years with you and wouldn't have had it any other way. Clients, business partners, friends and family love our Betty!!! Thank you for your tireless efforts and for always being there to help.

I also want to extend my heartfelt thanks to my business partners who have trusted me throughout the years. Your collaboration and support have been vital to our success. Thank you for your faith in me and for your ongoing partnership.

To my clients. Your continued trust and inspiration drive me to push myself to be better every day. Your stories, challenges, and successes have been a constant source of motivation. Thank you for allowing me to be a part of your life, as it is the reason why I wake up firing on all cylinders every day.

To you reading this book and the countless amount of people I am just as grateful for but were not specifically mentioned, I owe a debt of gratitude that words can scarcely express. Your love, support, and belief in me have made this work possible, and for that, I am eternally thankful.

Lastly and most importantly, I want to thank God. His guidance, blessings, and strength have been the cornerstone of my life and work. Thank you for Your grace and for giving me the perseverance to pursue my dreams. These past few years have been a whirlwind in every sense of the word and because of You, my entirety has been possible. I love you more than I could ever begin to love anything else and this glory goes to YOU, as I am a mere steward of Your Word and strive every day to reverse engineer my life to make You proud.

References

1. Baid, Gautam. *The Joys of Compounding: The Passionate Pursuit of Lifelong Learning.* New York City, Columbia Business School Publishing. 2020.
2. "How Often Do People Change Careers?" Indeed.com, updated June 24, 2022, https://www.indeed.com/career-advice/starting-new-job/how-often-do-people-change-careers.
3. "Building A Niche Advisory Business: It Takes 3 Years For People To Know, Like, And Trust," Kitces.com, Aug. 4, 2014, https://www.kitces.com/blog/building-a-niche-advisory-business-it-takes-3-years-for-people-to-know-like-and-trust/.
4. An accredited investor is one that is either worth $1,000,000 or more and/or one that makes $200,000 a year (if married, $300,000 a year) with reasonable certainty that they will continue to make that amount in the foreseeable future

5   "How to work best with 4 different types of learners," atlassian.com, Oct. 30, 2018, https://www.atlassian.com/blog/teamwork/how-to-work-4-different-learning-types.
6   "Listen up! Music may boost retail sales, expert says." CNBC.com, updated Nov. 4, 2014, https://www.cnbc.com/2014/11/01/listen-up-music-may-boost-retail-sales-expert-says.html.
7   "Onboarding and Development: Case Studies," Limra.com, accessed Jan. 11, 2024, https://www.limra.com/en/solutions-and-services/onboarding-and-development/case-studies/.
8   Poor Charlies' Almanack
9   "Median Home Prices By State 2024," Forbes.com, updated Oct. 24, 2023, https://www.forbes.com/advisor/mortgages/real-estate/median-home-prices-by-state.
10   "The Business Transition Handbook," thebusinesstransitionsherpa.com, accessed Jan. 11, 2024, https://thebusinesstransitionsherpa.com/the-business-transition-handbook/.

A free ebook edition is available with the purchase of this book.

To claim your free ebook edition:
1. Visit MorganJamesBOGO.com
2. Sign your name CLEARLY in the space
3. Complete the form and submit a photo of the entire copyright page
4. You or your friend can download the ebook to your preferred device

Print & Digital Together Forever.

Snap a photo

Free ebook

Read anywhere

www.ingramcontent.com/pod-product-compliance
Lightning Source LLC
Chambersburg PA
CBHW020905180526
45163CB00007B/2631